Behind the Veil of Economics

Books by Robert L. Heilbroner

The Essential Adam Smith
The Nature and Logic of Capitalism
Economics Explained
(with Lester C. Thurow)
Marxism: For and Against
Beyond Boom and Crash
The Economic Transformation of America
(with Aaron Singer)
Business Civilization in Decline
An Inquiry into the Human Prospect
Between Capitalism and Socialism
The Economic Problem
(with James K. Galbraith)
The Limits of American Capitalism
A Primer on Government Spending
(with Peter L. Bernstein)
The Great Ascent
The Making of Economic Society
The Future as History
The Quest for Wealth
The Worldly Philosophers

Robert L. Heilbroner

Behind the Veil of Economics

Essays in the Worldly Philosophy

W · W · NORTON & COMPANY

NEW YORK · LONDON

Published simultaneously in Canada by Penguin Books Canada Ltd., 2801 John Street, Markham, Ontario L3R 1B4.
Printed in the United States of America.

The text of this book is composed in Times Roman, with display type set in Janson. Composition and manufacturing by The Haddon Craftsmen, Inc.

Library of Congress Cataloging-in-Publication Data

Heilbroner, Robert L.
Behind the veil of economics.
Essays in the worldly philosophy
Includes index.
1. Capitalism. 2. Economics. I. Title.

HB501.H396 1988 330.12'2 87-20392

ISBN 0-393-30577-5

W. W. Norton & Company, Inc., 500 Fifth Avenue, New York, N.Y. 10110
W. W. Norton & Company Ltd., 37 Great Russell Street, London WC1B 3NU

2 3 4 5 6 7 8 9 0

Contents

Preface 7

1
Behind the Veil of Economics 13

2
Capitalism as a Regime 35

3
On the Future of Capitalism 63

4
The World of Work 80

5
The Problem of Value 104

6
Adam Smith's Capitalism 134

7
Schumpeter's Vision 165

8
Vision and Ideology 185

Index 201

Preface

HERE IS a collection of essays that discuss economics from an unaccustomed point of view. In the prevailing conception, economics is the study of our society as a "price system"—that is, a study of the manner in which the private and self-interested activities of individuals are given coherence and design by the workings of the market mechanism. This ancient and fascinating problem, for which Adam Smith supplied an answer in the workings of the Invisible Hand and Karl Marx in the laws of motion of capitalism, remains central to the analytic task of economics—but not central to its constitutive nature. It is what economics does, but not what economics is.

The latter question provides the focus of interest for the present book. As my title announces, I am more interested in economics as a veil that obscures our social understanding than as a technique for discovering how our society works. What does the veil obscure? That the price system is also a system of power; that the work of analysis is inescapably colored by ideology and initiated by untestable "visions"; that the object over which the veil is spread is not a collection of individuals but a specific social order to which we give the name capitalism. All this indicates the distance that separates my view of economics from that of the great majority of its contemporary practitioners, although not so much from that of Smith or Marx, or perhaps Schumpeter. It is to call attention to these classical connections that I have used as my subtitle *Essays in the Worldly Philosophy.*

A brief word about the genesis of the essays. Three major chapters, "Behind the Veil of Economics," "Schumpeter's Vision," and "Vision and Ideology" have been written specifically for this book. The other chapters have appeared in various publications, identified in footnotes. I have rid the essays of as much specialized language as possible, and where unfamiliar economic terms seemed proper, provided small asides to make them accessible to nonspecialists.* More important, I have rewritten, and in some cases refashioned various parts of the essays to fit more smoothly into the overall theme of the book that must have been subliminally, but was not yet consciously in my thoughts when the individual pieces were composed.

Yet I have also deliberately retained the separateness of these essays by permitting a certain degree of overlap among them. My hope is that these overlaps will add reinforcement and cogency to an argument that is, I fully recognize, outside the ambit (perhaps I should say beyond the pale) of ordinary economics. As I turn my ideas over and over with the reader, they should become more famil-

---

*Chapter 5, "The Problem of Value," is at a somewhat more technical level than the others. Noneconomists may wish to pass it by.

iar, and as a consequence easier both to grasp and to criticize.

It remains only to add with pleasure a few words of thanks. Ross Thomson, my colleague at the Graduate Faculty of the New School, patiently read drafts of key chapters and provided sympathetic but deep criticisms; I am particularly indebted to him. Henri Zukier, another colleague, provided much valued encouragement and very helpful guidance with respect to the psychoanalytic understanding of social behavior. Both Peter Bernstein, my esteemed lifelong friend, and Adolph Lowe, my venerable mentor, gave as always criticism that was as constructive as it was unsparing. David Gordon, Edward Nell, Anwar Shaikh and Allen Oakley have criticized one or another of these essays most helpfully. They are all absolved from further guilt. Last, I am happy to thank the Sloan Foundation for a grant that greatly speeded my research on Schumpeter's work. And in a class by herself I put my wife, who has sustained me with her love and affection.

Behind the Veil of Economics

1

Behind the Veil of Economics

WHAT IS economics?

The question seems pointless: Economics is the study of the economy. The economy, as everyone uses the term, comprises those activities and institutions that determine our material well-being. In the face of the obvious, is it not merely pedantry to ask what economics "is"?

In fact, however, far from being pointless, the question is illuminating, not to say disconcerting. This is in part the case because economics as the study of the economy contains premises and value judgments of which it is itself unaware. In chapters to come, we will examine economics as a belief system, an ideology. But there is another answer to the question of why it is important to look into the meaning of economics. It is that our involvement in the economy exerts a systematic distortion over our perception of what we call "economics." That is the veil to which my title refers. It is the thrall exerted by economic society itself—a thrall among whose many profound effects we must include the curious difficulty of defining an aspect of our social existences with which we are on terms of the most intimate familiarity.

There is a considerable history of controversy into the proper definition of economics, over which I shall pass in a lengthy footnote.[1] Instead, I shall move directly to a definition that will not only conform to the general understanding with which we began, but will also serve as an entree to the question-within-a-question that we wish to explore. *Economics, as I see it, is the process by which society marshalls and coordinates the activities required for its provisioning.*

To be sure, any list of such activities will vary depending on the time frame to which it is applied, insofar as

---

1. Economics has been caught between two respectively unsatisfactory definitions: an "objective" interpretation tied to the idea of wealth, and a "subjective" one focused on decision making. Both approaches run into trouble, the first because "objective" wealth cannot be described without reverting to the subjective criterion of utility; the second because the central placement of subjectivity widens economics to the point at which it becomes applicable to everything, and therefore empty of specific "economic" content. Recently, for example, Richard Posner has called for a "functional," not a "definitional" approach to economics: economics becomes identified with a certain "density" of analytic concepts, such as perfect competition, utility maximization, equilibrium, and the like. "When economics is 'defined' in this way," he writes, "there is nothing that makes the study of marriage and divorce less suitable a priori for economics than the study of the automobile industry or the inflation rate." This approach strikes me as containing one vitiating weakness: it leaves completely unbounded the domain of the "economy." I presume there *is* such a domain, distinguishable from, say, the domain of "marriage." If so, its decisive criteria must surely be included in the definition of that which describes or studies it—namely, economics. Richard A. Posner, "The Law and Economics Movement," *American Economic Review,* May 1987, p. 2. For a general overview, see Israel Kirzner, *The Economic Point of View* (1960), which seeks to define economics in subjective (purpose-directed) terms; and Maurice Godelier, *Rationality and Irrationality in Economics* (1972), which reviews the difficulties (adding those of purpose) from a Marxian viewpoint.

child- getting and rearing, or the reproduction of culture, are as necessary for long-term provisioning as immediate consumption or the replenishment of worn-out capital for shorter-term provisioning. But in drawing up the list, considerations of the short term take precedence over the long, in that society must live from day to day before it can endure from year to year. And in this crucial short-term focus there is always a fairly well-defined core of provision-related tasks that enables us to separate "the economy" from the larger "society." What is equally important to note, however, is that no matter how we define the boundaries of this economic sphere, it cannot be understood merely as a congeries of activities—hunting, farming, making steel, or whatever. It must also be perceived (as indeed must other, noneconomic spheres) as a congeries of activities under the guidance of some means of coordination and orchestration. As we shall see, it is this means, in its modern form, that gives to economics both its immediately comprehensible outward appearance and its elusive inner character.

I am certainly not alone in stressing the role of a coordinating mechanism as an essential element of "the economy." Indeed, conventional analysis depicts three such integrative means: Tradition, in which the orchestrating function is accorded to roles and responsibilities of kinship or other communal relations; Command, where the function is accorded to the will of some superior figure or institution, typically the state; and the Market, where the process is carried out principally by the interaction of self-interested individuals competitively seeking access to the workplace or to the purchasing power of the public.[2]

As a rough and ready method of distinguishing among integrative processes this conventional description is useful enough, especially insofar as it accords with the great separation of modes of production into primitive, imperial, and capitalist. One aspect of the tripartite division, must, however, be singled out for attention. It is the belief that the integrative process of the Market is entirely distinct from that of Tradition and Command. This distinction is mainly based on the voluntary character of the process of orchestration in market societies, where the marshalling and coordination of individual activity is entrusted to acts of exchange freely entered into by both buyer and seller, not by duties and obligations imposed by the weight of custom or authority. Market societies therefore appear to operate without the incentives and inhibitions of tradition or hierarchy. Market systems are commonly described as "price systems"—the words referring to standardized responses (rising prices inducing sellers to augment their activity and buyers to diminish theirs; falling prices the opposite) by which the uncoordinated actions of market participants are brought into harmony. In contrast to the responses of individuals under systems of tradition or command, those of market society are viewed as activities governed by freely undertaken rational calculations aimed at maximizing the well-being of the marketers.

---

2. I have used this terminology myself in *The Making of Economic Society* (1963). My general description of the economy as comprising ordered activities of provisioning follows Adolph Lowe, *On Economic Knowledge* (1965), I, 2.

It is understandable, then, that the integrative process of the market should appear to be of an entirely different kind from that of older systems. It is here, however, that I must take my departure from the conventional account, and begin to explore the implications of my title. For I have gradually come to see the market system as one in which the same underlying processes that assure discipline and order as those of older societies continue to exert their force, although in a manner that escapes our recognition. In making this assertion, I do not wish to minimize the reality, importance, or difference that a market system brings into social life, or to deny that elements of "rational" calculation absent from traditional and command societies play a decisive role in its operation. What I shall argue is that these powerful aspects of the market process throw a veil over other processes—a veil that obscures understandings and recognitions that, were they present, would cause "economics" as well as market societies to look very differently from the way they do.

II

Let me begin to argue my case by examining more carefully the coordinating processes in nonmarket systems. In these societies, as many anthropologists have noted, the acts of production and distribution appear as intrinsic elements in the sociopolitical life of these communities. What we call the economy is, in Polanyi's words, "embedded in non-economic institutions."[3]

---

3. Karl Polanyi, "Aristotle Discovers the Economy," in Geo. Dalton, ed., *Primitive, Archaic, and Modern Economies: Essays by Karl Polanyi* (1968), p. 86.

How embedded? For Polanyi the phrase means that the necessary acts of production and distribution are performed as part of the discharge of social obligations. But this description, unexceptional as far as it goes, does not go to the bottom of things. For it leaves unexamined the manner in which these social (no longer "economic") activities are called into being and dovetailed to fulfill the requirements of different societies. There is missing, in other words, the subjective element of motivation or behavior without which Polanyi's designation of "economic acts" as sociopolitical roles does not yet explain how the actors are induced to perform their necessary tasks.

Our analysis properly starts, then, by asking what forces are at work within the ties of reciprocity, kinship, duty, and the like that provide the order-bestowing mechanism of primitive, early state, and nonmarket social orders. Here I take my lead from the general literature of depth psychology and psychoanalytically inclined anthropology in identifying those forces as the psychic propensities and capabilities that arise from the socialization of the infant and child. The ability to behave in "adult" fashion, including the performance of socially designated roles, must in every society be traced back to the behavior-shaping process of socialization, in particular to the prolonged nurturant experience in which the psychological and biological givens of the human species-being are gradually given socially acceptable shape and form.[4]

---

4. The theme is generally diffused throughout the psychoanalytic literature. See in particular Erik H. Erikson, *Childhood and Society* (1963) and *The Life*

Two aspects of this universal and inescapable socialization process attract our immediate attention. The first is the development of the general capacity for "affect"—that ill-defined but universally recognized psychological capacity for identification, trust, sympathy, and love. It is affect that permits or encourages or even demands the cooperative association of individuals, and that makes the assumption of some form of interindividual, rather than autistic behavior, a necessary starting point for all social analysis. Equally important in understanding the orchestrating process is to explain the obedience or acquiescence necessary for the subordination of the individual to the social will, whether embodied in custom or command. Those traits also depend on the socialization process, where they emerge from the gradual acceptance and internalization of the parental frustration imposed on infants' and childrens' fantasies and drives. However sympathetically this frustration is imposed, it is universally present in the nurturant experience, where it becomes internalized and sublimated to form the basis for adult obedience and—as the delayed enactment of repressed infantile fantasies—for the pleasures of adult domination.

For our purposes it is only necessary to recognize that the experience of infantile helplessness, like the development of infant affect, plays an indispensable part in securing the orchestration of adult "economic" life. Of course

---

Cycle Completed (1982), ch. 2–3; and Sigmund Freud, *Group Psychology and the Analysis of the Ego* (1951), passim, as well as the works of psychoanalytically oriented anthropologists and sociologists.

such socialization processes vary from individual to individual and perhaps even more widely from culture to culture. Nonetheless, in all social organizations we can observe behaviors of cooperation and trust on the one hand, and of acquiescence (and its correlate, the expression of domination) on the other; and there is no other explanation for these crucial behavioral manifestations, on which all social orders depend for their continuance, other than the universal socialization experiences by which the primary drives and fantasies of the infant are given adult form.

The thrust of my general argument must now be clear. Provisioning arrangements, however structured, derive their behavior-shaping capability from the socialization of primal drives into the adult capacity to form positive associations based on affect, as well as hierarchical relationships based on obedience. This is a statement that seems self-evident when we examine the economic life of premarket societies where the coordination of all social activity is transparently under the influence of feelings of trust, or of domination and subordination. It is only when the organization of social life falls under the sway of the market—and tellingly, only within those areas of social life that do fall under the market's aegis—that the essential roles of affect and acquiescence seem to disappear. Economic life now appears to dispense with both trust and obedience, in that the market exerts its social pressure with a minimum of face to face contact and without any explicit show of force. The economy surfaces from its social surroundings as a "disembedded" process, an independent and autonomous realm of activity.

III

It is time now to consider the market mechanism itself as a means of social coordination, both to clarify the nature of its integrative power and its relation to systems of tradition and command.

Let us commence with the element of freedom—or rather, since freedom is a social condition and not an individual behavioral property, with the idea of individuation, i.e., the desire or capacity of individuals to seek lifeways other than those imposed on them by the prevailing structure of social interests. That such a drive to individuation also exists at a primary level (although its manifestation comes slightly later in the rhythm of infant maturation) seems well established by psychoanalytic investigation; and from all historical evidence, there seems no doubt that the life chances of the individual are vastly enlarged by the rise of market society.[5] On the other hand, we must not ignore the constrained behavior that is required to achieve this increase in autonomy. To be viable, market systems require conventionalized responses to the signals of price arrays and movements, and when those responses fail to evince their required "well-behaved" character—as in the case of "panics," or "destabilizing" expectations—market systems break down. Thus the gain in individual freedom must be set against a necessity for routinization of behavior in the very sphere of activity that officiates over the provisioning process. The motives of

5. On individuation see Erikson, *Life Cycle Completed;* also Eli Sagan, *At The Dawn of Tyranny* (1985), pp. 354–366.

economic "rationality" that replace those of tradition and command are *imperatives,* precisely as are the motives they displace. The thrust for individuation in the individual's social behavior—the expansion of his or her life chances—is accommodated at the cost of newly added constraints on his or her interactive behavior, taken in its entirety.

In this same spirit it is useful to recall that for all its historical association with freedom, market society—i.e., capitalism—does not appear as the spontaneous upwelling of a drive for individuation, but is at first imposed over earlier forms of social orchestration. The extension and generalization of exchange relationships does not come until the eighteenth and even nineteenth centuries, with the enforced commodification of labor and land, first vividly described by Marx. No one, reading of the manner in which dispossessed agricultural labor was forced into the early English mills, would describe this as a manifestation of freedom working its way in history.

Whatever the difficulties of comparing the objective constraints of tradition and command with those of the market, there is no doubt that a decisive change soon takes place in the manner in which social controls over behavior are *perceived.* In earlier societies the integration of the individual into the life of the community is clearly seen as arising from feelings of positive affect (family ties, friendship, communal observances, etc.), or under the duress of communal pressure (scorn, ostracism) or coercive authority. Once its transitional pains are past, the integrative mechanism in market society appears to use none of these pressures, and to rest solely on our free engagement with the transactional apparatus of society. The economy appears as an autonomous process, wholly independent of the society within which it operates.

At the center of this general perception lies the idea of *exchange.* The exact attributes of exchange are rarely spelled out by economists, but presumably involve the impersonal, affectless interchange of goods or services according to their value to the participants—i.e., without obedience or obligation to another. To the extent that this perception is true, it follows that the market is indeed a wholly new means of social orchestration. It is therefore essential that we inquire as deeply as possible into the nature of the exchange relationship.

IV

Let us start by contrasting the exchange relationship as it is practiced in market societies with interchanges in nonmarket society. Anthropologists warn us not to conflate the two. For example, exchange must be distinguished from gift giving, even though the latter almost always involves a return gift. Exchange is impersonal rather than personal and largely drained of erotic or other content, whereas gifts are invariably personal and highly charged with emotional significance. Exchange presumes a mensurational system that permits exact requital, whereas gifts, which also assume requital, are usually returned in more-than-full "measure." Finally, the gift relation appears in all societies, whereas the act of impersonal, "equal" exchange is visible only where the special institutions of the market society have emerged to accommodate it. Even barter, presumably the historical forerunner of exchange, "has never been a quantitatively important model of transaction in any past or present economic system about which we have hard information."[6]

These attributes of exchange bring us to consider the psychological basis for the exchange relationship, and to ask whether we can discover the prototype of the relations of exchange in the experiences of infancy and childhood. It seems clear that none exist. Specifically, the fundamental market criteria of *impersonality* and *equality of requital* have no basis in infant experience. An "impersonal" relationship with a parenting figure is a contradiction in terms or a pathological deformation; and the notion of giving and exchanging "equally valued" objects cannot be discovered until fairly late in the developmental sequence. All that can be said is that the sense of selfhood and the recognition of the autonomy of others—both essential psychological capacities for participation in a market system—unquestionably find their psychological bases in the successful negotiation of the infancy-childhood passage, but this very general statement applies to successful adult behavior in all societies, and sheds no light on the behavioral characteristics of exchange alone.[7]

Indeed, we catch some intimation of the "unnatural-

---

6. George Dalton, "Barter," *Journal of Economic Issues,* March 3, 1982, p. 185; see also Lewis Hyde, *The Gift* (1978); Polanyi, "Aristotle Discovers," pp. 88–93.

7. See Polanyi on "equality," "Aristotle Discovers," pp. 88–89. With respect to autonomy, it is of interest that Piaget dates the onset of ideas of justice from the seventh to eighth year. The criterion changes from that of obedience to *given* rules, to that of egalitarian principles from 7–8 to 11–12 years, followed by norms of equality tempered by equity. Jean Piaget, *The Moral Judgment of the Child* in *The Essential Piaget,* eds., H. E. Gruber and J. J. Voneche (1977), p 187.

ness" of the ideally impersonal exchange relationship in noting the difficulty we have in avoiding face-to-face or eye-to-eye contact with even the most trivial market encounters, such as vendors of subway or toll tokens, newspapers, etc. The frequency with which seller and buyer alike attempt to introduce affect into affectless transactions with phrases such as "Thank you," "Have a nice day," and the like; and the fleeting but real sense of incompletion we experience when such a vendor does not utter the softening phrase or when a buyer does not acknowledge receipt of his or her goods with a smile also testify to the need to compensate for the missing psychological ground beneath the pure exchange relationship.

From what basis, then, does the orchestrating means of the market draw its capacity to shape human behavior? The economist answers "self-interest" and "rational calculation." And in market behavior there are, of course, both a readily discernible motive of self-interest, whose psychological roots are perhaps deeper than any, and an equally evident guide of rationality—after all, homo oeconomicus is also homo sapiens.

Are these, then, the roots of exchange behavior? The answer must be sought partly in history, partly in psychology. Since we have seen that the exchange system does not spring up spontaneously in human society, we cannot assert that the instinct for self-preservation, disguised as Smith's drive to "better our condition," is the direct cause of the market's appearance. Rather, it seems more reasonable to accord to that instinct the energy needed to adapt ourselves to the psychological exigencies and difficulties of the exchange confrontation, once it arises to accommodate the demands of the capitalist order. The same seems to be the case with rationality. We have no evidence from the long premarket history of mankind of any drive to express the particular kind of rationality expressed in the exchange of "equivalents." As before, it seems more plausible that rational calculation becomes a mode of interaction to which we are driven after a market system has been established.

This is not, to be sure, the conventional answer to the question. Economists, who are not much given to probing the subterranean aspects of behavior, generally take for granted that "rational maximizing" is a natural, and deeply ingrained, attribute of humankind. Yet even at the most superficial level, this explanation entails serious problems. It is widely recognized that "rationality" is a question-begging as well as an elucidating term. Moreover, the assumption that behavior is dominated by an individualistic, even solipsistic mindset leads to dilemmas and impasses—the famous Prisoner's Dilemma in which self-interested participants conclude a less satisfactory bargain for themselves than would be reached if each guided his action by an other-minded view; or the problems of the Tragedy of the Commons—the overuse of resources—in which self-oriented behavior leads to destructive collective outcomes.

This has resulted in a recent widening of the behavioral assumptions necessary for an exchange system to include a consideration of the well-being of others, thereby introducing an "altruistic" element to the calculus of "self-interest." These changes have been introduced in part to allow the theory of an exchange system to embrace observed behavior that is clearly inconsistent with a wholly self-oriented conception of motivation—philanthropy, for example—and in part simply to bring the economist's perception of motivation closer to that of the psychologist or philosopher. These caveats apply with special relevance to the activities or attitudes required to support the generalization of "maximizing" behavior. If maximizing means gaining the largest possible pecuniary (or material) well-being, the assumption of rational maximizing implies that we will, whenever possible, rob the blind, engage in minor pilfering, and systematically undertip or fail to tip. Such behavior would increase our money income, while subjecting us at worst to warnings or scornful looks. To the extent that we do not behave in these ways, we are clearly not maximizing our material but our psychological well-being. However reasonable this behavior may appear, it renders the notion of "rational" maximizing nothing other than hewing to a cultural norm.[8]

In this context, Fred Hirsch has written on the usefulness of religion in providing the shared beliefs that make

8. Amartya Sen writes: "Central to [the] problem is the assumption that when asked a question, the individual gives an answer which will maximize his personal gain. How good is this assumption? I doubt that it is very good. ('Where is the railway station?' he asks me. 'There,' I say, pointing to the post office, 'and would you please post this letter for me on the way?' 'Yes,' he says, determined to open the envelope and check whether it contains something valuable." "Rational Fools," *Philosophy and Public Affairs,* v. 6 (1977), pp. 331–332. See also J. Hirshleifer: "Some willingness to forego selfish advantage, some element of genuine trust between trading partners or among business associates, almost always remains a necessity in the world of affairs." "The Expanding Domain of Economics," *American Economic Review,* Dec. 1985, p. 58 (see also pp. 55–56). An exceptionally interesting reformulation of economic motivation is to be found in Robert H. Frank, *Passions Within Reason,* forthcoming), from which I have borrowed some examples.

a certain amount of cooperative behavior *rational,* because such cooperation then becomes part of the expectations of all actors, which thereby raises its rewards and effectiveness for each. Religion persuades people to *act* altruistically, even if they are not *really* altruistic. "[I]nformal social controls in the form of socialized norms of behavior," Hirsch writes, "are needed to allow the market process itself to operate. These range from personal standards such as telling the truth to acceptance of the legitimacy of commercial contracts as a basis for transactions. An important aspect is implicit agreement on the sphere of market behavior; on what can be bought and sold, what interests may be pursued individually and collectively. These matters are recognized as of crucial importance in the establishment of a market economy, but as an underpinning for existing market practices they have been neglected in modern economic analysis. The social prerequisites of markets have been studied by sociologists rather than by economists, who have been generally content to leave it so."[9]

Perhaps even more profoundly than Hirsch, John Locke recognized the necessity for an affectual foundation underneath exchange society. As Joyce Appleby has pointed out, "Locke . . . understood well the fragile underpinnings of an exchange economy. Commerce was more than anything else a system of promises . . . ; if people could be expected to cheat or lie in pursuit of their profit, how could those great enterprises be undertaken that required confidence that others would perform their duty.

9. Fred Hirsch, *The Social Limits to Growth* (1983), p. 121.

Legislators, Locke wrote, would be well advised not to require oaths—such as in customs transactions, where they expect them to be broken—for 'Faith and Truth . . . is the great Bond of Society' . . ."[10]

I can do little better than to embroider on Locke. Market society, with its linchpin principle of impersonal, equal-valued exchange, presupposes the tacit but strong subscription of all to the existing law. If such a subscription were not generally observed, transaction costs would soar and the exchange system would be hopelessly encumbered by the need to inspect and verify each step in the exchange process, to assure one's physical safety in the exchange situation, etc. There are of course situations in which "exchange" is not supported and protected by these safeguards. The fact that these occurrences make the headlines as criminal practices and are generally regarded as a threat to the very preservation of economic life only testifies to the need for a powerful underpinning of norms—institutionalizations of primary affect—in what is ordinarily thought to be the impersonal realm of economic life.

V

But what of power? How can a system which offers its participants the option of not entering the transactional situation, or of withdrawing from it at any time, impose the will of some individuals on others?

Classical and Marxian economists find the answer to

10. Joyce Appleby, *Economic Thought and Ideology in Seventeenth-Century England* (1987), p. 188.

this question in the inequality of the class positions from which the main market agents—laborers and capitalists—enter the exchange arena. This is surely a key element in the discovery of power within the exchange situation. But at least two other less commonly recognized attributes of the market under capitalism also testify to its function as a system of power. The first is an unequal construal of the meaning of "property" when it refers to the means of production (land or capital) and when it refers to labor power—the ownership by the individual of his or her laboring capacity, including the precious right to withhold that capacity if desired. Although these property claims appear to be identical, they are not. For the right to claim the product of the means of production conjoined with labor power is entirely vested in the first owner, not in the second. The capitalist farmer owns the crop raised on his land and the capitalist manufacturer the output produced in his factory. In exchange for a wage payment, the worker surrenders all claims to this output, even though it would appear—and many conventional economists claim—that labor and capital as "factors of production" exist on an entirely equal conceptual footing, one with the other. Thus the uncontested ownership by capital of all value added is evidence that the market system incorporates a system of asymmetrical disposition of its product—a disposition that reflects the presence of social domination, however unrecognized, within its operations.

Second, there is the fact—celebrated but not appreciated by economists—of the "power" of market forces themselves. By this I mean that economists take for granted that the dispositions of the market will not be resisted by other means of material allocation, such as force. If men and women are unable to enter into successful market relations—whether as workers or consumers—it is assumed they will acquiesce in social defeat even though the enforcing agency is only the impersonal authority of the exchange mechanism itself. The assumption is amply borne out in reality: Only on the rarest and most desperate occasions do unsatisfied individuals attempt to disobey the market system by violating its dispensations. In the vast majority of cases, its provisioning arrangements are accepted without question; and the law, which silently stands behind the market, remains uninvoked—but not on that account unneeded..

The capacity of the market to secure acquiesence in a provisioning process in which the surplus automatically accrues to the property of only one class obviously makes the market mechanism an executive instrument for a particular social order, precisely as the dispositions of command or reciprocity make these systems the instruments for the reproduction of their respective social orders. Put as simply as possible, this is to say no more than that capitalisms, like tribal societies, imperial kingdoms, feudalisms, or socialist states, are at bottom regimes of power and privilege, built on the granite of family ties, community norms, and above all, on a deeply inculcated "habit of subordination."[11]

---

11. Smith, *Wealth of Nations* (1937), p. 532, 670. See also the searching discussion of coercion within market systems in C. E. Lindblom, *Politics and Markets* (1977), pp. 43–51, 107–108.

VI

It is time to return to the beginning. What is economics? Why does it appear so transparently clear, only to become on examination, so elusive and mystifying?

The answer, I think, is now at hand. Economics is the name we give to a process found in all societies as a precondition for existence. The process consists of both activities of production and distribution, and of the means for orchestrating these activities in accordance with the aims of the social order. This seems an appropriate place, however, to reflect on a double meaning of the word *economics*—namely, its reference both to the actual processes of provisioning, and to the ideas and beliefs by which we explain (and justify) those processes. In premarket systems this explanatory function is of minor importance, focused in the main on whatever tensions may be generated between the moral values of the society and its provisioning practices. Only in market societies does the explanation system attain the standing of a full-fledged *independent* study of social processes. As such, economics is patently the instantiation of the very illusions of autonomy enjoyed by the economic process itself. This illusion is supported, of course, because the market provisioning process rapidly attains a degree of complexity that demands specialized study. Economics then becomes the "science"—i.e., the empirical scrutiny and functional analysis—of market-directed behavior, while remaining an ideology—a belief system—insofar as it accepts as final the analysis of social movement in terms of unexamined "economic" forces.

In societies in which the provisioning process takes place under the aegis of tradition and command, we can easily see that its constitutive activities are embedded not only in the social routines of kinship or other obligations, but in the socialized psyches of the individuals who must carry out its routines. Economics in these societies is therefore completely reducible to, and indistinguishable from, social and political behavior. We may continue to speak of the "economy" of nonmarket societies, but we add nothing to our understanding by so doing.

Matters are different in exchange societies, of which capitalism is the only full-fledged example. There the provisioning process appears to be based on entirely different foundations than those of nonmarket systems. The changes wrought by the market mechanism are so great, and their impact on our consciousness so deep, that it becomes impossible to speak of this orchestration process without designating it as a special realm, quite divorced from tradition and command. This is all the more the case, as I have just said, insofar as the logic of market interactions acquires a complexity and a self-regulating character that endow the market system with "a life of its own." Economics thereby emerges as a discourse that is not only necessary for the analysis of capitalist dynamics, but also as the designation of a provisioning process that appears to have no intrinsic resemblance to those of its predecessor societies.

It is this last implicit—often explicit—assertion with which I take issue. There is no doubt that market behavior requires a degree of individuation and calculation that set it off from nonmarket societies. Nor is there any doubt that the market mechanism, contained within its capitalist socioeconomic order, generates a unique, largely self-directing, and history-shaping trajectory. Yet, as I have tried to show, at a sufficient distance capitalism can be seen as a system of provisioning whose psychodynamic underpinnings are exactly the same as those of other societies, however differently they may appear to its members, or however different may be the social outcomes to which they lead. Despite the unprecedented changes wrought by capitalism, despite the enormously enlarged sphere accorded to the play of self-interest and rationality, the forces of affect and obedience—the universal products of the socialization of humankind—continue to serve their ignored, but irreplaceable motivational function. Unsupported by these forces, the institution of exchange would be incapable of marshalling and coordinating the activities required for the provisioning of a social order. The "mechanism" of exchange is therefore not an integrative system free of affect and power, but a system that depends upon these ancient modes of behavioral control—incorporating them in ways of extraordinary complexity, unleashing from them a heretofore unknown social dynamic, ignoring their active and essential contribution, but depending on them all the same. There is therefore no mystery involved in the assertion that economics is fundamentally an embodiment of the forces of morality and politics, interpreted broadly. The mystery, rather, resides in our difficulty in perceiving this.

wealth on an unprecedented scale, a capacity to which Marx and Engels paid unstinting tribute in *The Communist Manifesto.* It is important to understand that the wealth amassed by capitalism differs in quality as well as quantity from that accumulated in precapitalist societies. Many ancient kingdoms, such as Egypt, displayed remarkable capacities to gather a surplus of production above that needed for the maintenance of the existing level of material life, applying the surplus to the creation of massive religious or public monuments, military works, or luxury consumption. What is characteristic of these forms of wealth is that their desirable attributes lay in the specific use values—war, worship, adornment—to which their physical embodiments directly gave rise. By way of decisive contrast, the wealth amassed under capitalism is valued not for its specific use values but for its generalized exchange value. Wealth under capitalism is therefore typically accumulated as *commodities*—objects produced for sale rather than for direct use or enjoyment by their owners; and the extraordinary success of capitalism in amassing wealth means that the production of commodities makes possible a far greater expansion of wealth than its accumulation as use values for the rulers of earlier historical formations.

Both Smith and Marx stressed the importance of the expansion of the commodity form of wealth. For example, Smith considered labor to be "productive" only if it created goods whose sale could replenish and enlarge the national fund of capital, not when its product was intrinsically useful or meritorious. In the same fashion, Marx described the accumulation of wealth under capitalism as a circuit in which money capital (M) was exchanged for commodities (C), to be sold for a larger money sum (M′), in a never-ending metamorphosis of M–C–M′.

Although the dynamics of the M–C–M′ process vary greatly depending on whether the commodities are trading goods, or labor power and fixed capital equipment, the presence of this imperious internal circuit of capital constitutes a prime identificatory element for capitalism as a historical genus. As such, it focuses attention on two important aspects of the genus. One of these concerns the motives that impel capitalists in their insatiable pursuit. For modern economists the answer to this question lies in "utility maximization," an answer that generally refers to the same presumed attribute of human nature as that which Smith called the "desire of bettering our condition."[3] The unappeasable character of the expansive drive for capital suggests, however, that its roots lie not so much in these conscious motivations as in the gratification of unconscious drives, specifically the universal infantile need for affect and experience of frustrated aggression. Such needs and drives surface in all societies as the desires for prestige and for power and domination. From this point of view, capitalism appears not merely as an "economic system" knit by the appeals of mutually advantageous exchange, but as a larger cultural setting in which the pursuit of wealth fulfills the same unconscious purposes as did the thirst for military glory or the celebration of personal majesty in earlier epochs. I call such a setting a "regime," both to convey the sheer force at its center,

3. Adam Smith, *Wealth of Nations,* p. 324.

and to make clear the gulf between such a vision and that of the impersonal "system" dear to conventional economics.[4]

A second general question raised by the centrality of the M–C–M′ circuit concerns the manner in which the process of capital accumulation organizes and disciplines the social activity that surrounds it. Here analysis focuses on the institutions necessary for the circuit to be maintained. The crucial capitalist institution is generally agreed to be private property in the means of production (not in personal chattels, which are found in all societies). The ability of private property to organize and discipline social activity does not however lie, as is often supposed, in the right of its owners to do with their property whatever they want. Such a dangerous social license has never existed. It inheres, rather, in the right accorded its owners to *withhold* their property from the use of society if they so wish.

This negative form of power contrasts sharply with that of the privileged elites in precapitalist social formations. In these imperial kingdoms or feudal holdings, disciplinary power is exercised by the direct use or display of coercive force, so that the bailiff or the seneschal are the agencies through which economic order is directly obtained. The social power of capital is of a different kind—a power of refusal, not of assertion. The capitalist may deny others access to his resources, but he may not force them to work with them. Clearly, such power requires circumstances that make the withholding of access an act of critical consequence. These circumstances can only arise if the

---

4. See Heilbroner, *Nature and Logic,* ch. 2.

general populace is unable to secure a living unless it can gain access to privately owned resources or wealth. Capital thus becomes an instrument of power because its owners can establish claims on output as their quid pro quo for permitting access to their property.

Access to property is normally attained by the relationship of "employment" under which a laborer enters into a contract with an owner of capital, usually selling a fixed number of working hours in exchange for a fixed wage payment. At the conclusion of this "wage-labor" contract both parties are quit of further obligations to one another, and the product of the contractual labor becomes the property of the employer. This is, of course, the asymmetry of property claims we encountered in our previous chapter. From this product the employer will pay out his wage obligations and compensate his other suppliers, retaining as a profit any residual that remains.

In detail, forms of profit vary widely, and not all forms are specific to capitalism—trading gains, for example, long predate its rise. Explanations of profit vary as a consequence, but as a general case, it can be said that all profits depend ultimately on inequality of economic position. When the inequality arises from wide disparities of knowledge, or access to alternative supplies, profits typically emerge as the mercantile gains that were so important in the eyes of medieval commentators, or as the depredations of monopolistic companies against which Adam Smith inveighed. When the inequality stems from differentials in productive capability, we have the quasi rents to which such otherwise different observers as Marshall and Schumpeter attribute the source of capitalist gain. And when the inequality is located in the market relationship between employer and worker it appears as the surplus value central to Marxian and, under a different vocabulary, to classical political economy. As Smith put it, "Many a workman could not subsist a week, few could subsist a month, and scarce any a year without employment. In the long-run the workman may be as necessary to his master as his master is to him; but the need is not so immediate."[5]

This is not the place to enter into a discussion of these forms of profit, all which can be discerned in modern capitalist society. *What is of the essence under capitalism is that gains from whatever origin normally accrue to the owners of capital, not to workers, managers, or government officials.* This is a clear indication both of the difference of capitalism from, and its resemblance to earlier social formations. The difference is that product itself now flows to owners of property who have already remunerated its producers, not to its producers—usually peasants in precapitalist societies—who must then "remunerate" their lords. The resemblance is that both arrangements channel a social surplus into the hands of a superior class, a fact that again reveals the nature of capitalism as a regime, not merely a system of rational exchange.

Thus we can see that the successful completion of the circuit of accumulation represents a political as well as an economic challenge. The attainment of profit is necessary for the continuance of capitalism not alone because it replenishes the wherewithal of each individual capitalist

---

5. Smith, *Wealth,* p. 66.

(or firm), but because it also demonstrates the continuing validity and vitality of the principle of M–C–M′ as the basis on which the formation can be structured. Profit is for capitalism what victory is for a regime organized on military principles, or an increase in the number of adherents for one built on a proselytizing religion.

II

Capitalism as a social order whose organizing principle is the ceaseless accumulation of capital cannot be understood without some appreciation of the historic changes that bring about its appearance. In this complicated narrative, it is useful to distinguish three major themes. The first concerns the transfer of the organization and control of production from the imperial and aristocratic strata of precapitalist states into the hands of mercantile elements. This momentous change originates in the political rubble that followed the fall of the Roman empire. There merchant traders established trading niches that gradually became loci of strategic influence, so that a merchantdom very much at the mercy of feudal lords in the ninth and tenth centuries became by the twelfth and thirteenth centuries an estate with a considerable measure of political influence and social status. The feudal lord continued to oversee the production of the peasantry on his manorial estate, but the merchant, and his counterpart the guild master, were organizers of production in the towns, of trade between the towns, and of finance for the feudal aristocracy itself.

The transformation of a merchant estate into a capitalist class, capable of imagining itself as a political, not just an economic force required centuries to complete and was not, in fact, legitimated until the English revolution of the seventeenth and the French revolution of the eighteenth centuries. The elements making for this revolutionary transformation can only be alluded to here in passing. A central factor was the gradual remonetization of medieval European life that accompanied its political evolution. The replacement of feudal social relationships, mediated through custom and tradition, by market relationships knit by exchange worked steadily to improve the wealth and social importance of the merchant against the aristocrat. This enhancement was accelerated by many related developments—the inflationary consequence of the importation of Spanish gold in the sixteenth century which further undermined the rentier position of feudal lords; the steady stream of runaway serfs who left the land for the precarious freedom of the towns and cities, placing further economic pressure on their former masters; the growth of national power that encouraged alliances between monarchs and merchants for their mutual advantage; and yet other social changes.

The overall transfer of power from aristocratic to bourgeois auspices is often subsumed under the theme of the rise of market society—that is, as the increasing organization of production and distribution through purchase and sale rather than by command or tradition. This economic revolution, from which emerge the "factors of production" that characterize market society, must however be understood as the end product of a *political* convulsion in which one social order is destroyed to make way for a new social order. Thus, the creation of a large propertyless labor force—the prerequisite for the appearance of labor power as a commodity that would become enmeshed in the M–C–M′ circuit—requires a disruptive social change that begins in England in the late sixteenth century with the dispossession of peasant occupants from communal land, and does not run its course until well into the nineteenth century. In similar fashion, the transformation of feudal manors from centers of social and juridical life into real estate, or the destruction of the protected guilds before the unconstrained expansion of nascent capitalist enterprises embody wrenching sociopolitical dislocations, not merely the smooth diffusion of preexisting economic relations throughout society. It is such painful rearrangements of power and status that underlay the "great transformation" out of which capitalist market relationships finally arise.[6]

A second theme in the historical evolution of capitalism emphasizes a related but distinct aspect of political change. Here the main emphasis lay not so much in the direct organization of production, as in the separation of a traditionally seamless web of rulership, extending over all activities within the historical formation, into two realms, each concerned with different functions within the whole. One of these realms involved the exercise of the traditional political tasks of rulership—mainly the formation and enforcement of law, and the declaration and conduct of war. These undertakings continued to be entrusted to the existing state apparatus which retained (or

---

6. Karl Polanyi, *The Great Transformation* (1957), Part II.

regained) the monopoly of legal violence and remained the center of authority and ceremony. The other realm was limited to the production and distribution of goods and services—that is, to the direction of the material affairs of society, from the marshalling of the work force to the amassing and use of the social surplus. In the fulfillment of this task, the second realm also extended its reach beyond the boundaries of the territorial state, insofar as commodities were sold to and procured from outlying regions and countries that became enmeshed in the circuit of capital.

The formation of these two distinct realms was of epoch-making importance for the constitution of capitalism. The creation of a broad sphere of social activity from which the exercise of traditional command was excluded bestowed on capitalism another unmistakable badge of historic specificity, namely the creation of an "economy," a semi-independent state within a state and also extending beyond its borders.

This in turn has brought two remarkable consequences. One of these is the establishment of a political agenda unique to capitalism, in which the relationship of the two realms becomes a central question around which political discussion revolves. In this discussion the overarching unity and mutual dependency of the two realms tend to be overlooked. The organization of production is generally regarded as a wholly "economic" activity, ignoring the political function performed by the wage-labor relationship in disciplining the work force in lieu of bailiffs and seneschals. In like fashion, the discharge of political authority is regarded as essentially separable from the operation of the economic realm, ignoring the provision of the legal, military, and material contributions without which the private sphere could not function properly or even exist. In this way, the presence of two realms, each responsible for part of the activities necessary for the maintenance of the social formation, not only gives to capitalism a structure entirely different from that of any precapitalist society, but also establishes the basis for a problem that uniquely preoccupies capitalism, namely the appropriate role of the state vis-à-vis the sphere of production and distribution.

More widely recognized is the second major effect of the division of realms in encouraging economic and political freedom. Here the capitalist institution of private property again takes center stage, this time not as a means of arranging production or allocating surplus, but as the shield behind which designated personal rights can be protected. Originally conceived as a means for securing the accumulations of merchants from the seizures of kings, the rights of property were generalized through the market into a general protection accorded to all property, including not least the right of the worker to the ownership of his or her own labor power.

Now the wage-labor relationship appears not as a means for the subordination of labor but for its emancipation, for the crucial advance of wage labor over enslaved or enserfed labor lies in the right of the working person to deny the capitalist access to labor power on exactly the same legal basis as that which enables the capitalist to deny the worker access to property. There is, therefore, an institutional basis for the claim that the two realms of capitalism are conducive to certain important kinds of freedom, and that a sphere of market (or other non-state) ties may be necessary for the prevention of excessive state power. This is surely an important part of Smith's celebration of the society of "natural liberty," and has been the basis of the general conservative endorsement of capitalism. Unquestionably, the greatest attainments of human liberty thus far attained in organized society have been achieved in certain advanced capitalist societies. One cannot, however, make the wider claim that capitalism is a sufficient condition for freedom, as the most cursory survey of modern history will confirm.

A third theme in the evolution of capitalism calls attention to the cultural changes that have accompanied and shaped its institutional framework. Much emphasis has been given to this theme in the work of Weber and Schumpeter, both of whom stress the historic distinctions between the essentially rational—that is, means–ends calculating—culture of capitalist civilization, compared with the "irrational" cultures of previous social formations.

Here it is important to recognize that rationality does not refer to the *principle* of capitalism, for we have seen that the impetus to amass wealth is only a sublimation of deeper-lying nonrational drives and needs. Rationality refers to the *behavioral paths* followed in the pursuit of that principle. The drive to amass capital cannot be reduced to mere accountancy any more than can the drive for power. The increasingly "logical" aspect of the search for wealth is the sign not of its increasingly rational nature, but of the abstract nature of exchange value which makes possible—

indeed, which enforces—measurements and calculations that would be impossible in regimes where power is not denominated in money. The drive for wealth is not qualitatively different from that for glory, but the pressures exerted by the marketplace direct and constrain it in ways that have no counterpart in premarket regimes. Capitalism is therefore distinguishable in history by the predominance of a prudent, accountant-like comparison of costs and benefits, a perspective discoverable in the mercantile pockets of earlier formations, but highly uncharacteristic of their ruling elites. "I prefer to have no inventory of my possessions, so that I may be less sensible of a loss," writes Montaigne.[7]

The cultural change associated with capitalism goes further, however, than the rationalization of its general outlook. Indeed, when we examine the general culture of capitalist life we are most forcibly struck by an aspect that precedes and underlies this rationalization, namely the presence of an ideological framework that contrasts sharply with that of precapitalist formations. I do not use the word *ideology* in a pejorative sense, as denoting a set of ideas foisted on the populace by a ruling order in order to manipulate it, but rather as a set of belief systems to which the ruling elements of the society themselves turn for self-clarification and explication. In this sense, ideology expresses what the dominant class in a society sincerely believes to be the true explanations of the questions

---

7. Montaigne, *Essays* (1979), p. 204. See also Schumpeter, *Capitalism, Socialism, and Democracy* (1947), ch. 11; Max Weber, *Protestantism and the Rise of Capitalism* (1930), passim.

it faces. It is the "vision" whose importance will steadily come to the fore as we proceed.

That which is characteristic of the ideologies of earlier formations is their unified and monolithic character. In the ancient civilizations of which we know, an all-embracing world view, usually religious in nature, explicates every aspect of life, from the workings of the physical universe, through the justification of rulership, down to the smallest details of social routines and attitudes. By way of contrast, the ideology that emerges within capitalism is made up of diverse strands, more of them secular than religious and many of them in some degree of conflict with other strands. By the eighteenth century, and to some degree before, the explanation system to which capitalist societies turn with respect to the workings of the universe is science, not religious cosmology. In the same manner, rulership is no longer regarded as the natural prerogative of a divinely chosen elite but perceived as "government"—that is, as the manner in which "individuals" create an organization for their mutual protection and advancement. Not least, the panorama of work and the patterns of material life are perceived not as the natural order of things, but as a complex web of interactions that can be made comprehensible through the teachings of political economy, later economics. The individual threads of these separate scientific, political-individualist, and economic belief systems originate in many cases before the unmistakable emergence of capitalism in the eighteenth century, but their incorporation into a skein of culture provides yet another identifying theme of the history of capitalist development.

Within this skein, the ideology of economics is obviously of central interest for economists. A crucial element of this belief system involves changes in the attitude toward acquisitiveness itself, above all the disappearance of the ancient concern with good and evil as the most immediate and inescapable consequence of wealth-gathering. As Albert Hirschman has shown, this change was accomplished in part by the gradual reinterpretation of the dangerous "passion" of avarice as a benign "interest," capable of steadying and domesticating social intercourse rather than disrupting and demoralizing it. Other crucial elements of understanding were provided by Locke's brilliant demonstration in *The Second Treatise on Government* (1690) that unlimited acquisition did not contravene the dictates of reason or Scripture, and by the full pardon granted to wealth-seeking by Bentham who demonstrated that the happiness of all was the natural outcome of the self-regarding pursuit of the happiness of each.[8]

The problem of good and evil was thus removed from the concerns of political economy and relegated to those of morality; and economics as an inquiry into the workings of daily life was thereby differentiated from earlier inquiries, such as the reflections of Aristotle or Aquinas, by its explicit disregard of their central search for moral understanding. Perhaps more accurately, the constitution of a "science" of economics as the most important form of social self-scrutiny of capitalist societies could not be

---

8. Albert Hirschman, *The Passions and the Interests* (1977); John Locke, *The Second Treatise on Government,* ch. 5; Jeremy Bentham, *Principles of Morals and Legislation* (1790; 1970).

attempted until moral issues, which defied the calculus of the market, were effectively excluded from the field of its investigations.

III

This conception of capitalism as a historical formation with distinctive political and cultural as well as economic properties derives from the work of those relatively few economists interested in capitalism as a "stage" of social evolution. In addition to the seminal work of Marx and the literature that his work has inspired, the conception draws on the writings of Smith, Mill, Veblen, Schumpeter, and a number of sociologists and historians, notable among them Weber and to a lesser extent Braudel. The majority of present-day economists do not use so broad a canvas, concentrating on capitalism as a market system, with the consequence of emphasizing its functional rather than its institutional or constitutive aspects.

In addition to the characteristic features of its institutional "nature," capitalism can also be identified by its changing configurations and profiles as it moves through time. Insofar as these movements are rooted in the behavior-shaping properties of its nature, we can speak of them as expressing the logic of the system, much as conquest and dynastic alliance express the logic of imperial systems built on the principle of imperial rule, or the relatively changeless self-reproduction of primitive societies expresses the logic of societies ordered on the basis of kinship, reciprocity, and adaptation to the givens of the physical environment.

The logic of capitalism ultimately derives from the pressure exerted by the expansive M–C–M′ process, but it is useful to divide this overall force into two categories. The first of these concerns the "internal" changes impressed upon the formation by virtue of its necessity to accumulate capital—its metabolic processes, so to speak. The second deals with its larger "external" motions—changes in its institutional structure or in important indicia of performance as the system evolves through history.

The internal dynamics of capitalism spring from the continuous exposure of individual "capitals" to capture by other capitalists. This is the consequence of the disbursement of capital-as-money into the hands of the public in the form of wages and other costs. Each capitalist must then seek to win back his expended capital by selling commodities to the public, against the efforts of other capitalists to do the same. This process of the enforced dissolution and uncertain recapture of money capital in the circuit of accumulation gives rise to the pressure of competition that is the social outcome of generalized profit-seeking. We can see, however, that competition cannot be adequately described merely as the vying of suppliers in the marketplace. As both Marx and Schumpeter recognized, competition is at bottom a consequence of the mutual encroachments bred by the capitalist drive for expansion, not of the numbers of firms contending in a given market.

The process of the inescapable dissolution and problematical recapture of individual capitals now gives rise to the logical activities designed to protect these capitals from seizure. The most readily available means of self-defense is the search for new processes or products that will yield a competitive advantage—the same search that also serves to facilitate the expansion of capital through the development of new markets. Competition thus reinforces the introduction of technological and organizational change into the heart of the accumulation process, usually in two forms: attempts to cheapen the cost of production by displacements of labor by machinery (or of one form of fixed capital by another); or attempts to gain the public's purchasing power by the design of new forms of commodities. As a consequence, one of the most recognizable attributes of capitalist "internal" dynamics has been its constant revolutionizing of the techniques of production and its continuous commodification of material life, the sources of its vaunted capacity to change and elevate living standards.

A further internal change also arises from the expansive pressures of the core process of capital accumulation. This is a threat to the capacity of capital as a whole to extract a profit from the production of commodities. This tendency arises from the long-run effect of rising living standards in strengthening the bargaining power of labor versus capital. There is no way in which individual enterprises can ward off this threat by cutting wages, for in a mobile, competitive society they would thereupon lose their ability to marshal a work force. Their only protection against a rising tendency of the wage level is to substitute capital for labor where that is possible. For the system as a whole, the ability to hold down the bargaining power of labor must therefore hinge on a generalization of individual cost-reducing efforts through the system-wide displacement of labor by machinery, or by the direct use of government policies to maintain a profit-yielding balance between labor and capital, or by systemic failures—"crises"—that create generalized unemployment. Whether attempted by deliberate policy or brought about by the outcome of spontaneous market forces, capitalists' efforts to hold wages to levels compatible with adequate profits thus become a key element in the internal dynamics of the system.

A final attribute of the internal logic of capitalism must also be traced to its core process of accumulation. This is the achievement of a highly adaptive method of matching supplies against demands without the necessity of political intervention. This cybernetic capacity is surely one of the historical hallmarks of capitalism, and is regularly contrasted with the inertias and rigidities of systems in which tradition or command (planning) must fulfill the allocational task. A critique of the successes and failures of the market system cannot be attempted here. Let me only emphasize that the workings of the system itself derive from institutional attributes whose genesis we have already observed, namely the establishment of free contractual relations as the means for social coordination; the establishment of a social realm of production and distribution from which government intervention is largely excluded; the legitimation of acquisitive behavior as the social norm; and activating the whole, the imperious search for the enlargement of exchange value as the active principle of the historical formation itself.

IV

From the metabolism of capitalism also emerges its larger "external" motions—the overall trajectory often described as its macroeconomic movement, and the configurational changes that are the main concern of institutional economics. It may be possible to convey some sense of these general movements if we note three general aspects characteristic of them.

We have already paid heed to the first of these, the tendency of the capitalist system to accumulate wealth on an unparalleled scale. Some indication of the magnitude of this process emerges in the contrast between the increase in per capita GNP of developed (capitalist) and less developed (noncapitalist) countries:

GNP per capita (1960 dollars and prices)[9]

	Presently developed countries	Presently less developed countries
Around 1750	$180	$180–190
Around 1930	$780	$190
Around 1980	$3,000	$410

After our lengthy discussion of the central role of accumulation within capitalism it does not seem necessary to relate this historic trend to its institutional base. Two

9. Paul Bairoch in Just Faaland, *Population and the World Economy in the 21st Century* (1982), p. 192.

somewhat neglected aspects of the overall increase in wealth seem mentioning, however. The first is that the increase in per capita GNP includes both augmentations in the volume of output and an extension of the M–C–M′ process itself into the social world. This is manifested in a continuous implosion of the accumulation process *within* capitalist societies—the process of the commodification of material life to which we earlier referred—and its explosion into neighboring noncapitalist societies.

This explosive thrust calls attention to the second attribute of the overall expansion of wealth. It is that capital, as such, knows no national limits. From its earliest historic appearance, capital has been driven to link its "domestic" base with foreign regions or countries, using the latter as suppliers of cheap labor power or cheap finished commodities, or as markets for the output of the domestic economy. The consequence has been the emergence of self-reinforcing and cumulative tendencies toward strength at the Center to which surplus is siphoned, and weakness in the Periphery from which it is extracted. The economic dimensions of this global drift are immediately visible in the previous table. This is the basis for what has been called the "development of underdevelopment" as the manner in which ancient patterns of international hegemony are expressed in the context of capitalist relationships.[10]

---

10. Gunnar Myrdal, *Rich Lands and Poor* (1957), Part I; Paul Baran, *The Political Economy of Growth* (1957), chs. 5–7.

We turn next to a different overall manifestation of the larger logic of capitalist development—its changes in institutional texture. There have been, of course, many such changes in the long span of Western capitalist experience. Nonetheless, two changes deserve to be singled out, not only because of their sweeping magnitude and transnational occurence, but because they have deeply altered the evolutionary logic of the system itself. These have been the emergence within all modern capitalisms of highly skewed size distributions of enterprise, and of very large and powerful public sectors.

The general extent of these transformations is sufficiently well known not to require detailed exposition here. Suffice it to illustrate the trend by contrasting the largely atomistic composition of manufacturing enterprise in the United States at the middle of the nineteenth century with the situation in the 1980s, when seven-tenths of all industrial sales were produced by one-hundredth one percent of the population of industrial firms. The enlargement of the public sector is not so dramatic, but is equally unmistakable. During the present century in the United States, its size (measured by all government purchases of output plus transfer payments) has increased from perhaps 7.5 percent of GNP to over 35 percent, a trend that is considerably outpaced by a number of European capitalisms.

The first of these two large-scale shifts in configuration can be directly traced to the pressures generated by the M–C–M′ circuit. The change from a relatively homogeneous texture of enterprise to one of extreme disparities of size is the consequence not only of differential rates of growth of different units of capital, but of defensive business strategies of trustification and merger, and the winnowing effect of economic disruptions on smaller and weaker units of capital. There is little disagreement as to the endemic source of this transformation in the dynamics of the marketplace and the imperative of business expansion.

The growth of large public sectors is not so immediately attributable to the accumulation process proper, but rather, results from changes in the logic of capitalist movements after the concentration of industry has taken place. Here the crucial change lies in the increasing instability of the market mechanism, as its constituent parts cease to resemble a honeycomb of small units, individually weak but collectively resilient, and take on the character of a structure of beams and girders, each very strong but collectively rigid and interlocked. It seems plausible that this rigidification of the system was the underlying cause of the increasingly disruptive crises that appeared first in the late nineteenth century and climaxed in the Great Depression of the 1930s; and it is widely accepted that the growth of the public sector mainly owes its origins to efforts to mitigate the effects of that instability or to prevent its recurrence.

This brings us to the last general aspect of capitalist development, namely the tendency for interruptions and failures to break the general momentum of capital accumulation. Perhaps no aspect of the logic of capitalism has been more intensively studied than these recurrent failures in the accumulation process. In the name of stagnation, gluts, panics, cycles, crises, and long waves a vast literature has emerged to explain the causes and effects of intermittent systemic difficulties in successfully negotiating the passage from M to M′. The variables chosen to play strategic roles in the explanation of the phenomenon are also widely diverse: the saturation of markets; the undertow of insufficient consumption; the technological displacement of labor; the pressure of wages against profit margins; various monetary disorders; the general "anarchy" of production; the effect of ill-considered government policies; and still others.

Despite the variety of elements to which various theorists have turned, a common thread unites most of their investigations. This is the premise that the instabilities of capitalist growth originate in the process of accumulation itself. Even theorists who have the greatest confidence in the inherent tendency of the system to seek a steady growth path, or who look to government intervention (in modern capitalism) as the main instability-generating force, recognize that economic expansion tends to generate fluctuations in the rate of growth, whether from the "lumpy" character of investment, volatile expectations, or other causes. In similar fashion, economists who stress instability rather than stability as the intrinsic tendency of the system do not deny the possibility of renewed accumulation once the decline has performed its surgical work: indeed, Marx, the most powerful proponent of the inherently unstable character of the M–C–M′ process, was the first to assert that the function of crisis was to prepare the way for a renewal of accumulation.

In a sense, then, the point at issue is not whether economic growth is inherently unstable, but the speed and efficacy of the unaided market mechanism in correcting its instability. This ongoing debate mainly takes the form of sharp disagreements with respect to the effects of government policy in supplementing or undermining the corrective powers of the market. The failure to reach accord on this issue reflects more than differences of informed opinion with regard to the consequences of sticky wages or prices, or ill-timed government interventions, and the like. It should not be forgotten that from the viewpoint of capitalism as a regime, interruptions pose the same threats as did hiatuses in dynastic succession or breakdowns of imperial hegemony in earlier formations. It is not surprising, then, that the philosophic predilections of theorists play a significant role in their diagnoses of the problem, inclining economists to one side or the other of the debate on the basis of their general political sympathies with, or antipathies to, the regime, rather than on the basis of purely analytic considerations.

V

All the foregoing aspects of the system can be traced to its inner metabolism, the money–commodity–money circuit. This is much less the case when we now consider the overarching pattern of change described by the configuration of the social formation as a whole as it moves from one historic "period" to another.

Traditionally these periods have been identified as early and late mercantilism; preindustrial, early, and late industrial capitalism; and modern (or late, or state) capitalism. These designations can be made more specific by adumbrating the kinds of institutional change that separate one period from another. These include the size and character of firms (trading companies, putting-out establishments, manufactories, industrial enterprises of increasing complexity); methods of engaging and supervising labor (cottage industry through mass production); the appearance and consolidation of labor unions within various sectors of the economy; technological progress (tools, machines, concatenations of equipment, scientific apparatus); organizational evolution (proprietorships, family corporations, managerial bureaucracies, state participation). David Gordon has coined the term "social structure of accumulation" to call attention to the changing framework of technical, organizational, and ideological conditions within which the accumulation process must take place. Gordon's concept, applied to the general problem of periodization, emphasizes the manner in which the accumulation process first exploits the possibilities of a "stage" of capitalism, only to confront in time the limitations of that stage which must be transcended by more or less radical institutional alterations.[11]

The idea of an accumulation process alternately stimulated and blocked by its institutional constraints provides an illumining heuristic on the intraperiod dynamics of the system, but not a theory of its long-run evolutionary path. This is because not all national capitalisms make the transitions with equal ease or speed from one social structure to another, and because it is not apparent that the pressures of the M–C–M′ process push the overall structure in

11. David Gordon, "Systems of Accumulation and Long Economic Cycles," in *Processes of the World System,* eds. Terence Hopkins and Immanuel Wallerstein (1980).

any clearly defined direction. Thus Holland at the end of the seventeenth century failed to make the leap beyond mercantilism, and England in turn in the second half of the nineteenth century failed to create a successful corporate capitalism. In this regard it is interesting that the explanatory narratives of the great economists apply with far greater cogency to the evolutionary trends within periods than across them—Smith's scenario of growth in *The Wealth of Nations,* for instance, containing no suggestion that the system would move into an industrial phase with quite different dynamics, or Marx's depiction of the laws of motion of the industrialized system containing no hint of its worldwide evolution toward a state-underwritten structure. Although the inner characteristics of the M–C–M′ process enable us to apply the same generic designation of capitalism to its successive species-forms, it does not seem to be possible to demonstrate, even after the fact, that the transition from one stage to another had to be made, or to predict before the fact what the direction of institutional adjustment will be.

But while history forces on us a salutary caution with regard to long-term pronouncements, it is interesting to note that all the great economists have envisaged an eventual end to the capitalist period of history. Smith describes the accumulation process as ultimately reaching a plateau when the attainment of riches will be "complete," followed by a lengthy and deep decline. Ricardo and Mill anticipate the arrival of a "stationary state" which Mill foresees as the staging ground for a kind of associationist socialism. Marx anticipates a series of worsening crises, each crisis serving a temporary rejuvenating function, but

3

On the Future of Capitalism

As will be immediately apparent, this chapter is not an essay at all, but an interview.[1] I include it here, even though it repeats many themes of the previous chapter, because it translates these themes from their rather high level of abstraction into a much more specific and historic context. It is, if you will, a look behind the veil of economics into today's state of affairs.

Q. Are the present economic difficulties a product of policy or are they in some way inherent in the economic system?

A. We have an unfortunate conjuncture of two currents, both of which are creating difficulties: one, the policies of Reaganomics which are now being partially reversed; the other, visible in many countries besides our own, what seems to be the end of an era, the falling away of the

1. Reprinted with permission of the publisher, M.E. Sharpe, Inc., 80 Business Park Drive, Armonk, New York 10504, from the Nov./Dec. 1982 issue of *Challenge*. The interviewer was Myron Sharpe.

momentum of the fifties, a change in general outlook, and the threat of potential financial crisis. We live at a time when we have to cope both with the immediate exigencies of an ill-thought-through political-economic program and the deeper ones of a global crisis.

Q. When you say crisis, what do you mean? How is this crisis related to policy and how is it related to longer-run trends?

A. I think more and more that the historic trajectory of capitalism displays a certain kind of pattern in which opportunities for investment appear, are eagerly exploited, and are gradually exhausted. After this the system decelerates and seeks new channels into which to pour its energies. This is in some ways, I suppose, like the Kondratief cycle, except I have never liked the idea that there is a 25-year timing mechanism behind it. That there are successive periods of dynamism followed by periods of exhaustion seems to me to be borne out by history. There haven't been terribly many of these periods—the industrial revolution, the great railroadization period, the long booms of the pre-World War I and post-World War II eras. Since the 1970s we have been again in a typical post-boom, thrashing around while we seek some new avenue of expansion.

Q. You are talking about something cyclical and, therefore, we will have growth and prosperity again. Is this a valid implication?

A. It is very hard to say. I was recently reading a book, *Dynamics of Global Crisis,* in which four scholars of the left, Immanuel Wallerstein, Andre Gunder Frank, Samir Amin, and Giovanni Arrighi, write their projections for the future. I was struck by the fact that virtually all of them anticipate a picking up of momentum again beginning roughly in the 1990s. These days it seems to be very fashionable among the left, which not so very long ago was talking about the imminent replacement of capitalism with some other system, to think in terms of a continuing momentum of the system once it makes its necessary institutional adjustments. I myself think that just as the left in the past has been much too quick to call finis, now it may be much too quick to anticipate continuous regeneration.

Q. Are you suggesting that you disagree with that point of view?

A. I am agnostic. I do believe that the system shows a number of signs of having outrun the institutional structure that generates momentum, accumulation, and growth. I think that the capitalist economies will have to make some major readjustments before that momentum is restored. But I am not such a determinist as to say that this will happen. It may happen; it may not. I believe more and more that one essential quality of capitalism is its capacity to adjust and adapt. There is a very good likelihood that at least some capitalisms in the world will find new institutional structures, but I'd be the last one to say that this must happen in all capitalisms everywhere. In the United States, in particular, I am dismayed at the moment by what seems to be the singularly negative position with regard to changing aspects of the system which stand in the way of renewed growth.

Q. Why should we talk about this in terms of so large a concept as the capitalist system? Why don't we just talk about it in terms of mistakes in monetary, fiscal, and various other policies? Why can't we explain the whole of our present economic difficulties in those immediate pragmatic terms?

A. I'd give two answers to that. One easy answer is that the symptoms of trouble and disarray or even disorganization seem to be global rather than just located in Reaganomics country, and that they surfaced before Reagan's policies began to bite. The second is that I think the necessary concept to bring order into these currents and crosscurrents of history is the organizing idea of capitalism as a regime. Capitalism as a regime has more than one identifying characteristic. But its central, driving characteristic is surely its need constantly to accumulate, to seek avenues for the investment of capital in order to create more capital. In slightly different terms this is a formulation every businessman would agree with. It is the profit motive, expansion, growth. Using another vocabulary, it is the belief in the primary role of investment that the economics profession in general takes. The imperative for capital formation, growth—accumulation is the term that I prefer—is central because capitalism depends on that in order to reproduce and preserve its entire sociopolitical structure.

Q. Do you think there are particular advantages in looking at present problems in your framework?

A. I find a central thread missing from the endless discussions about what we should be doing—namely, an absence of any historical appreciation of the nature of the system. People write about our time of trouble—they may even use the word "crisis"—as if capitalism were a changeless or eternal state of affairs which has somehow temporarily lost its bearings. One of the reasons why I shy away from too exclusive an emphasis on policy is that it assumes that the underlying process is basically all right—it has just been turned aside or thwarted because of some poorly conceived operation on the part of the government. I prefer to think of capitalism as a regime which, however adaptive, is nonetheless always focused on one central necessity, namely, to generate more capital—if you will, more wealth. That is a process which for long periods seems to run effortlessly and smoothly and successfully. Then the institutions that permit and generate that accumulation—forms of business organization, for example, or relations between the state and the economy, or business and labor—seem to lose their effectiveness and the system chokes up and has to seek new channels for expansion—sometimes new technological channels, sometimes new geographical areas, sometimes new institutions. Crises occur when existing institutions lose their stimulative and guiding capability. It then becomes clear that there has to be some major restructuring. For instance, the great crisis over which Keynesian economics initially presided was that of finding an institutional answer to underemployment and underinvestment. When the depression broke out there was no conception, and certainly no institutional possibility, of using the government as a growth-generating mechanism. The crisis of our time is not that crisis; it is rather one of reestablishing forward momentum in a period when we have no institutional means of capping the inflationary potential that growth generates. Sometimes capitalism has to seek new private institutions, such as the construction of big business out of small business; sometimes it has to seek new government institutions. Today I think it must move in both a "statist" and "laborist" direction.

Q. You realize that most economists do not think about our problems this way. They deal with problems of inflation, unemployment, production, productivity, and pragmatically try to develop policies for specific problems. Sometimes the policies are right and sometimes they are wrong. If they are wrong we hope that they will be changed. What is the advantage of looking at the present difficulties the way you do, as opposed to the way the majority of the economics profession does?

A. I think the advantage of a historical perspective is that it helps one imagine alternative formulations for capitalism, whereas a perspective that takes the existing structure for granted tends to inhibit the reach of that imagination. To take the case in point, the view that capitalism is a system of surplus generation capable of highly adaptive forms with regard to the mix between what is called the "government" sector and the "private" sector makes understandable the idea that the system may be drifting in a direction in which that mix is likely to change in favor of government. This then appears as a more thinkable, less outrageous possibility than if one takes the position that whatever the mix is today somehow gives once and for all the boundaries of the system. Looking at capitalism historically, recognizing the extraordinary changes that divide 1890 from 1850, and 1930 from 1890, and that may well divide 2010 from 1970, helps one recognize the degree to which widely differing configurations are within the possibilities of the system.

Q. You've told me that you've revised your ideas about the nature of capitalism over the last several years. How would you describe that revision?

A. For thirty years now I have been ruminating about this system in which we live. I have changed my mind about it more than once, and more and more have tried to find some way of formulating what I think its innermost nature is. The reason I do this is partly because I am interested in economic history and the history of economic thought, but really because it seems to me that a failure to appreciate the "nature" of the system leads one to myopic views about what the system is, and then to very shallow recommendations about what it can do, what it can't do, what its difficulties are, and so on. What appalls me most in so much that I read about our troubles is the failure to appreciate the nature of the beast, its possibilities, its limitations. When I began to get interested in this problem, a long time back, I defined capitalism in very simplistic terms. I certainly was not the only person to do so. But those stock formulations did not adequately convey the nature of the system, which I now see as having three elements in its quintessential being. One of those elements, to repeat, is the overwhelming, internally generated need constantly to accumulate capital. All social systems above the level of what we call "primitive society" generate surpluses, whether we speak of ancient China, ancient Egypt, or ancient kingdoms of Africa. What is different about capitalism as a surplus-generating system is that it is the only system that invests its surplus, not in articles of personal or public luxury and adornment, but in the means to achieve more wealth. A wealthy capitalist nation is not a nation characterized by bigger pyramids or better cathedrals or even better roads or bigger cities than any other nation. It is a nation that has more capital. That capital may be computer factories, toy factories, automobile factories. But the common measure is their capacity to generate more surpluses. The capitalist system is made up of entrepreneurs, businessmen, and capitalists, who are constantly searching to enlarge their own capital-generating capacity. What for? Because that's how power and prestige are gained by these individuals. But that is only one of the elements of capitalism.

The second very important element is that capitalism splits an aspect of society which was unitary until capitalism arose. That unitary aspect is the exercise of authority over the system as a whole, as regards both the maintenance of its hierarchical structure and the continuance of its material provisioning. If you look at ancient Egypt, feudal Europe, traditional China, you see a bailiff appropriating bushels of grain from the fields, some of which the landlord will keep and some of which he will pass on to his overlord. Is the landlord acting as a political personage or as an economic personage? Is he exercising authority or some sort of allocatory function? The answer is that he is doing both at the same time. There is no sphere of politics as such, perhaps war and diplomacy aside. There is no sphere of economics as such, even though markets exist. The actions of all the central players in these ancient regimes form an indissoluble whole, both a means of continuing political hierarchy and a means of assuring the generation of surplus and the continuance of the system. Only in capitalism, which begins after the mercantile stratum separates out, do we begin to have the extraordinary division of society in two: a political realm that presumably has nothing to do with economics any more, a government that doesn't carry on any production; and an economic realm that carries on production but doesn't do any governing. Then you first have a mercantile class—later on an industrial capitalist class—whose only job is to make money, or to carry on trade, or to do production, but which isn't supposed to do any governing at all. No businessman in the world, *qua* businessman, considers himself a governor or a political figure. In the political stratum, no administrator, no representative, no judge, considers himself to be a member of the productive echelon of society.

And yet, despite the appearance under capitalism of these dual realms, the political and the economic, both realms carry on both functions; one openly, one covertly. The political realm openly conducts the business of politics: it rules, it gives laws, it enforces the law, it practices diplomacy and war. But at the same time it provides absolutely essential support for the private sector. It carries on economic activities which, were they privatized, would result in losses. It builds roads, infrastructure, it does things essential for the country which cannot be undertaken by the economic sphere because, by the rules of the game, these don't make money.

Now you take the economic part. The economic sphere carries on a very important political task, which it doesn't recognize as being political, namely, assuring the essential discipline that maintains the work process. In feudal times there's branding and clipping and a bailiff with a whip. In capitalism, nobody whips the man who doesn't show up for work. Nobody assures discipline in the sense that the feudal lord does. The disciplinary function, and it is there, God knows—the function of getting people to do work they don't particularly like and to do it regularly—is provided by *the system,* in the form of the need to gain income.

The third distinguishing feature of capitalism is that it has no monolithic explanation of how things are in the form of state religion, as earlier systems did—an explanation that begins with the cosmos and that comes down to the nature of rule, the legitimacy of the emperor, the place of priest, the place of peasant, the continuum into which all fall as part of the divine order. Under capitalism that monolithic belief disintegrates into at least three different belief systems. You have a system of explanation about how this new thing called "the economy" works. Economics provides that explanation. You have a new set of explanations about how rulership is exercised. That is called political theory. Third, you have a belief system that organizes the meaning of the world around us, which is no longer seen as sacred and divine. It is explained in terms of science. So capitalism is characterized by diverse, complex systems of belief, quite different from the unified ones in the old sphere.

Now, to me, it is essential to see capitalism as a complex entity in which the failure to gain surplus brings a systemic crisis of one kind or another; in which economic and political authority is wielded in very mystifying ways, ways that even those who wield it do not fully understand; and in which there are confluences and sometimes conflicts of economic, political, and scientific beliefs that collectively define the imagination of the system. It seems to me that this conception frees one from the shackles of a view of capitalism that sees it only in terms of "freedom," or just in terms of maximizing subject to constraints, or of individuals contending for scarce resources.

Q. What conclusions do you draw from all this?

A. This view of mine leads to many kinds of questions that are overlooked by people who are just "policy-minded." One of them is how to bound the system, considered as a regime. The old socialist question about socialism in one country has now been matched by the question of capitalism in one country. Is capitalism always and essentially, as Immanuel Wallerstein says, a world system? Is capitalism by its very nature a process of uneven development, with advanced regions and backward regions?

Q. What do you mean by capitalism in one country?

A. I mean, is the conventional conception of capitalism too narrow in that it fails to ask whether accumulation isn't essentially a process of draining wealth out of weak strata or regions into the hands of strong strata or regions, and that this process takes place without any particular regard to national boundaries? This raises a whole set of questions that are left unasked by conventional economists.

Still another question that my perspective opens up is whether or not the entire debate about public and private isn't an obscurantist approach to the actual reality of the system. Historically speaking, if a thousand years from now capitalism is understood as a curious chapter in history in which there was a bifurcation of "political" and "economic," each carrying on an overt and a covert set of activities, people will regard with amazement that the participants in the system argued so vociferously about what was private and what was public; that they failed to see that the private sector made essential contributions to the polity, namely, the preservation of economic order and discipline, and that the public sphere made essential contributions to the ongoing momentum of the economy, namely, the provision of what we call infrastructure.

Q. But there is a distinction between infrastructure and other types of goods and services, isn't there?

A. In some ways, of course. But they cannot be wholly separated. In order to produce automobiles, one must have roads to run them on and socialized individuals to go into the factories. The government provides the roads and the government schools the workers. Take away the schools and take away the roads, and you cannot have an automobile industry.

Q. That's true, but there is a kind of tacit, if not explicit, agreement that government will provide the roads and private industry will provide the automobiles.

A. The only reason why the government provides the roads and private industry provides the automobiles is that it is in the nature of the existing conventions that you can sell automobiles and you can't sell roads. If you could imagine these conventions changing in some fashion, such that you could sell road service and you couldn't sell cars, then you could be absolutely sure that there would be a General Roads Corporation and a Department of Automobiles.

Q. You raised the question about capitalism as a world system. Are you accepting the thesis that the developed countries depend on exploitation of the underdeveloped for their accumulation process?

A. I remember that in the fifties, when I first began to be interested in underdevelopment, I heard a few murmurs from the left that underdevelopment was a condition of as well as a product of capitalism. I felt that this was an absurd misrepresentation. But I begin to see what is meant by the never very cogently put argument. It is that all world imperial systems are webs of power. All of them have centers and peripheral regions. Capitalism is also a world system in the same sense that the Incas were a world system, though the world they knew was narrow, or that China or ancient Egypt or Rome were world systems. Except that capitalism does not have a political capital like Rome. The capital of capitalism is the geographical location of highly developed regions where we find the strategic nuclei of the commodities that are produced.

Q. You seem to be implying that development itself depends on underdevelopment.

A. I am not sure about the phrase "depends on." I think the two are simultaneous aspects of a unitary process and I think I can best show it in an instance. When you think of the Roman Empire, it is very easy to picture the relations of the center to the periphery. Here was Rome and there was Gaul, and from Gaul wheat and other products flowed into Rome. Everybody understands that. It was true of China. It was true of India. From the provinces there flowed in, either in cash or kind, the tribute which made possible the enormous temple complexes, palaces, arenas, armies, and so forth. I think this is true of capitalism too, with a curious difference. Although you still have a rich center and a poor periphery, the lines of national division are drawn by political events that are no longer so intimately tied in with the extraction of surplus as they were in the unitary empires of the past. If you can imagine today's map of capitalist nations without any national boundaries, you have something like two or three Roman Empires. You would have the poor regions on the outside, Peru and the Mexican backwaters, Southeast Asia, and so on, sending their tribute in cash or kind into the rich European, Japanese, and American centers. If you could imagine no national boundaries and just the economic system, you would see centripetal flows that would not be so different from what you see under the Roman flow. It's enormously more complicated because just as national capitalism has a political and economic bifurcation, so international capitalism is overlaid with a jigsaw puzzle of national boundaries.

Of course, one might argue that today there is a return flow of goods, which wasn't true in Roman times. But is it an *equal* return? Conventional economics says yes. Radical economics says no. I think the radical view is right. How else shall we explain the widening gap between the center and the periphery?

Q. But the Greco-Roman system was based on slavery, which was a system of very low labor productivity. The capitalist system is based on industrial equipment. It's a system of very high productivity. It produces, to use the phrase that you have been using, enormous surpluses in comparison with the surpluses that the Greco-Roman system produced. The surpluses that were taken in from the periphery of the Greco-Roman system were very important to it because of its own low productivity. Are the surpluses taken in by the developed capitalist countries in any way equivalent in importance?

A. That's a very difficult question and I'm somewhat of two minds about the answer. On the one hand I see the inflow from cheap labor and materials in the periphery making possible the generation of profits that accrue to the center. I see cheap labor in Taiwan eventually making it possible for General Motors to equip its automobiles with inexpensive radios which, if they were produced in Detroit, would cost many times those which are produced in Taiwan. So I do think that the difference between the advanced and the backward areas is an important part of the continuous generation of surplus to the system. On the other hand, I also think that modern capitalism is characterized by a Schumpeterian gale of technology, by the winning of technological rents, by the milking of markets simply by being there first with a new product. This is of enormous importance for capitalist countries and generates some of this tremendous intersystemic rivalry which is so difficult for us to cope with. But in this war of technology the periphery plays no major role.

Q. In the race between adaptation and disaster, who's winning?

A. As between modern-day state socialism and capitalism, capitalism is winning. But that does not interest me as much as the limits of adaptation of capitalism. I have written, half tongue-in-cheek, half seriously, that socialism is the last stage of capitalism. That brings a smile to everybody's face. But what I mean by socialism is Western bourgeois ideas of individual freedom, participation, democracy, equality. All these words that we like so much are, it seems to me, associated with the rise of the bourgeois culture of the eighteenth and nineteenth centuries. Capitalism is thus moving in a generally "socialist" direction. However, history is not a railroad track and it would be foolish to say that all capitalist nations will, in the fullness of time, become Scandinavias. They will not. Countries have their cultural and political differences. I am quite sure that countries can find branch lines from the main track, maybe disastrous ones like "national socialism" or Fascism, or maybe simply ones that end in a kind of cultural or political stagnation or a morass of indecision and blindness. I feel myself that the United States is right now in such a position of indecision and blindness, not knowing where we are and not knowing where to go. We might easily move to the right. But for me the more interesting question is how far capitalism might move in a socialist direction.

Is there some meaning to socialism beyond Sweden? What's over the hill after capitalism has adopted all the participatory and democratic institutions and changes that it can adopt? I am impressed by Branko Horvat's book, *The Political Economy of Socialism,* in which he says that the meaning of socialism lies ultimately in the complete lodging of decision-making and responsibility for the labor process in labor, and the complete lodging of political responsibility in citizens, and the breaking down of all the structures, whatever they are called, capitalist, communist, or just bureaucratic, that inhibit direct expression of self-responsibility. Such a definition of socialism lies well beyond anything that we now have.

Q. Do you think you could run General Motors by a democratic vote of all the participants?

A. I don't think a General Motors is imaginable under a kind of Horvat-like definition of socialism. I think it would require a much smaller scale of both productive and political units of action. I don't think you could have vast economic units. This immediately raises the question, "Can you have vast political units? Can you have the nation state?" This is a question that Horvat doesn't really deal with. It may be that the nation is in some way the ultimate barrier that has to be transcended before something like socialism may be reached. That is, socialism and the nation state may be mutually incompatible. Indeed, that seems to me the only way that freedom and socialism can be ultimately reconciled.

4

The World of Work*

IS THE SUBJECT of economics imaginable without the concept of work? I think not. Yet, although economists write at great length about work-times, work-rates, work-choices, and the like, they do not reflect much on the idea of work itself. Perhaps this is because work embraces so much of human experience—joy and despair, fulfillment and anesthesia, creativity and drudgery—that it seems beyond the sober consideration of a social scientist. Everyone admits that work is no doubt the inescapable starting point for social inquiry—if only we knew where to start.

I shall suggest such a starting point in this essay by examining work from a somewhat unaccustomed vantage point—a vantage point from which work appears on a different axis than that of the pains and pleasures of toil. I shall look at work as a fundamental expression of subordination and its opposite—freedom. From this perspective the great issues of ethics and economics, of psychology

---

*This paper was originally delivered at a meeting of the Council of Scholars of the Library of Congress and published as "The Act of Work" by the Library in 1985.

treks, individual or collective privations and sacrifices. There are as well applications of energy and aesthetic intelligence applied to the making of shelters, wearing materials, ornaments, and weapons. There are activities that are enjoyed and others that are endured. Nevertheless, by the criteria of work as we know it—criteria that I will shortly come to—there is no work in the societies of the !Kung and the Pygmy, the Trobrianders and the Yir-Yoront of Australia, the peoples of the Amazon forest and the Arctic icelands. If we can take it to be the case that these are the vanishing remnants of earliest human society—a form of human life portrayed in Genesis—it follows that there was indeed no work in Paradise.

What can it mean to say that primitive man does no work? I mean that the tasks associated with the physical sustenance of the group are not distinguished by organization or esteem from other tasks and activities also required to maintain collective life, such as the rearing of children, the participation in various social decisions, the transmission of culture, and the like. In this skein of activities, the performance of those that we would call *work* carry no special identifying characteristic that sets them apart. The activities are not carried out under any one's supervision or command. They have no particular priority or pressure about them. They carry neither the great freight of honor or achievement nor any great stigma of dishonor or failure. Their pace is normally not hurried or timed—save, of course, when the moment comes to strike: then the arrow must fly or the harpoon be launched at the exact moment. Perhaps most important, they are not carried out for any extrinsic purpose. There may be differences in rewards between those who excel and those who are poor at, or who shirk, their tasks of hunting or gathering, but the performance of these tasks does not bring social advancement any more than the performance of other tasks such as cooking food or building huts.

In the face of such differences, can we call these activities *work?* For lack of a sufficiently discriminatory vocabulary we subsume them under that term. But we can see that they are so radically different in motive, rationale, organization, and social control that the term is inappropriate by our standards. We say that it is a lot of work to take care of a child, but we do not mean the same as when we say there is a lot of work at the office. In the same way, the Yir-Yoront use the same word for work and play,[3] although I imagine that they too distinguish between hunts and games. Only in their case the overall designation is one of pleasure (utility, in the economist's vocabulary), not its opposite.

II

The idea that a society can exist without work is disturbing because it implies that work is the product of society and not the other way around, as we ordinarily imagine. That is, indeed, basic to my argument, but before pursuing it, I must add a few words with respect to the material life of primitive society. The last thing in the world I wish to do is to romanticize primitive existence. Life in such a society would be unbearable for modern men and women, not alone for a lack of creature comforts

---

3. Sahlins, *Stone Age Economics,* p. 64.

and intellectual stimulation, but for the absence of that very thing we call work. Nonetheless, if we are to consider work at its roots, primitive society is where we must begin.

Two aspects of this workless life must be brought to center stage. The first is that a world without work is a world without material wealth. It is not, anthropologists tell us, a world without material well-being—even without a sense of affluence—but it is assuredly a world virtually bare of stocks of consumption goods or capital equipment.[4] Life is lived in a kind of trusting surrender to nature. Very little time generally separates the collection or production of food or raw materials from their use, so that there is little stimulus to develop the arts of indirect, "roundabout" production that require manmade equipment of an elaborate kind.

The second aspect of this workless existence is of even greater importance. It is that this leisurely and confident mode of production-and-consumption rests on an essential social condition—the absence of any "property" in nature. I put the word in quotation marks because there are many kinds of property. All of them, however, have one feature in common—they cede to some members of society the right to withhold from the rest of society the use of these things in which they have property rights. Were the fruits of the earth or its animals the property of some members of the primitive group, the domestic mode of production could not exist, for the tasks that households carry out for their own material subsistence would then depend on securing the permission of the own-

---

4. Ibid., p. 34f.

ers of nature, not merely the silent acquiescence of nature itself.

III

Our theme of subordination and freedom thus begins to appear as the central relationship that defines the act of work itself. Work cannot be depicted solely in terms of objectively defined tasks. The essence of work is that these tasks are carried out in a condition of subordination imposed by the right of some members of society to refuse access to vital resources to others.

The consequences of this subordination touch many facets of work, as we shall see. First, however, we must inquire a little further into the advent of this epochal change. Work as we now understand it appeared some five thousand years ago with the coming of civilization, a term by which I mean not merely the systematic accumulation of material wealth and high culture but the displacement of the domestic mode of production by various kinds of centralized modes. In these modes, the control over resources does indeed become a defining feature of society, usually lodged in the prerogatives of godlike kings and surrounding retinues of priests and nobles, who defend their rights with military force, laws, and punishments.

It is impossible to exaggerate the significance of this extraordinary change in the human condition. It is perhaps the greatest inflection point in social experience, whose mythic representation is the expulsion from the Garden of Eden. Thereafter, the Bible tells us, mankind lives by the sweat of its brow. As we can interpret that exodus, the change describes the end of the era of self-regulated, socially unimpeded access to the bounties of nature, and the commencement of the human history of work.

We do not know why mankind made this leap from primitive freedom and equality to subordination and inequality. Population growth may have forced neighboring bands into conflicts that ended in sub- and superordination. Climatic events, such as the Ice Age, may have pushed horsed nomads into contact with, and then supercumbency over, agriculturalists—according to the German historian Rüstow, the possible origin of the myth of the conquering centaur.[5] Or perhaps the relatively benign advent of social stratification became the less benign institution of social domination.[6] The matter remains obscure. What is certain, however, is that the change occurs as a fulcral moment for societal evolution, bringing with it the precious achievements and horrendous pains of civilized existence.

Let us look for a moment at these pains and pleasures as they affect the new social activity called work. The necessity to obtain the permission of the owners of resources to gain access to them has universally entailed one main condition: those needing access have agreed to surrender a portion of their work-product to those who controlled those resources. Thus the act of work, as the manner in which human energy is concerted under civilization, is inextricable from exploitation. That is a

---

5. Alexander Rüstow, *Freedom and Domination* (1980), p. 29.

6. Morton Fried, *The Evolution of Political Society* (1967), pp. 224–26. See also Henri Claessen and Peter Skalnik, *The Early State* (1978), pp. 3–8.

word before which we tend to wince. But in early civilization it is not difficult to see it nakedly apparent and coercively enforced. The figures of the rent-racked peasant and the abused slave are inextricable from the centralized mode of production. Exploitation is thus the economic face of centralized political and military power. It is the dark netherworld of civilization.

It is also, of course, the necessary condition for the achievement of civilization, at least so far as its material triumphs are concerned. As we have seen, the time and energy spent on production are matters of small importance for those engaged in the domestic mode of production, but they become matters of supreme importance for those who are the beneficiaries of others' work. The labor hours commanded by ruling classes are an index of their power, so that the sheer volume of work time increases. The work energies at their disposal become, in addition, the means by which nature's gifts may be collected, stored, refined, and displayed for their enjoyment. Without work, in the exploitative sense that I have stressed, there would be no pyramids, Great Walls, temple complexes, cathedrals, irrigation systems, or road systems—nor the high culture that arose within and from these material underpinnings.

Work takes on a second aspect in the centralized mode of production because it is channeled into activities that require not merely skill but education, not merely judgment but equipment. These activities create the new social category of the craftsman—the skilled worker—who emerges in civilization as a special kind of worker. The craftsman produces wares that the ruler admires and wants, but he is dependent on the ruler for his livelihood. Thus architecture, armaments, engineering; sculpture, music, literature; jewelry, raiment, even cuisine give rise to their practitioners—their skills as remarkable as those of the hunter, but their status much more ambiguous. On the one hand, the finished work of the craftsman is admired; on the other, his social place remains inferior.

Before these contradictory significances of work, ancient observers of society stood in considerable confusion. Socrates was accused of inculcating a slavish attitude in his pupils by teaching that work was not necessarily demeaning—a mistake that his best pupil, Plato, and Plato's best pupil, Aristotle, did not repeat.[7] This denigration of work—even skilled work—can only be understood from the viewpoint of the genesis of work, with its intrinsic principle of submission to the power of another. It is impossible not to admire the product of the craftsman, but dangerous to admire the person, for that would be to accord honor to submission or worse, to criticize the legitimacy of the very principle of stratification itself.

Much of the subsequent tortuous history of the moral evaluation of work involves efforts to reconcile the contradictions of labor as a value-creating activity and as an ignoble station. It is here, of course, that Christianity plays its important subversive role, extolling work *because* of its submissiveness, the humble attitude of the worker symbolizing the appropriate attitude for the servant of God. I shall not attempt to review that lengthy narrative with its climactic triumph of a "work ethic" under Luther and

7. Hannah Arendt, *The Human Condition* (1958), p. 82, n. 7.

Calvin but will content myself with pointing out that the whole issue of the moral and social ambiguity of work would be incomprehensible if work itself were not originally tainted by its inherent submission. It is against this long-forgotten social condition that the ethical struggles to justify work must be understood.

IV

Let us now continue with our theme by moving from *homo laborans,* the special concern of the Church, and *homo faber,* the favorite of the Court, to a new hero of work, *homo oeconomicus,* the discovery of the emerging arbiters of social values, the political economists.

The early economists were essentially concerned with explaining the nature and logic of a new mode of production that was beginning to shoulder aside older centralized modes by the eighteenth century—the mode of capitalism. Not surprisingly, they placed the act of work, and its integration into the social whole, at the very center of their explanations, and for this very good reason: Of all the changes that capitalism brought, none was more striking than the manner in which it marshalled and allocated labor. The relationships of lord and peasant, master and slave, the main forms of work-submission for five thousand years, disappeared, and in their place rose that of the waged worker, entering into a contractual engagement of "employment" through a network of society-embracing markets.[8]

---

8. The entry of waged labor as an important form of work relationship dates only from about the seventeenth or even early eighteenth centuries. See Jan de Vries, *The Economy of Europe in an Age of Crisis* (1976), pp. 95, 248.

Adam Smith called this new mode of organizing production a society of "perfect" or "natural" liberty, for men entered into the crucial relationship of employment on the basis of their own decisions to do so and terminated that relationship on the same self-determined basis. In a word, they chose what they wanted to do; and decided whether to do it on the terms at which work was offered. Never mind the obvious limitations of this choice, of which we shall speak later. The initial thing to grasp is how revolutionary—how free—was this condition of work compared with slavery or serfdom, or even with the milder form of apprentice to a guild master.

Yet, in the light of our historical perspective we can see that it was not "perfect" or "natural" freedom. For whereas the individual was indeed free to seek work as he or she wished, in the vast majority of cases this still required crossing over the barrier of property to gain access to land or equipment. Presumably the owners of resources under capitalism exacted a toll from those who sought access to them, as had been the case ever since the domestic mode disappeared. But what was the nature of this toll?

The answer obviously lay in the rents and profits that accrued to property. But a mystification arose under capitalism, in that rents and profits were not coercively seized as had formerly been the case. There was no bailiff in the fields of the capitalist farmer to separate the owner's grain from the peasant's. No overseer exercised expropriative powers at the factory gate, taking the capitalist's share of the product. On the contrary, the worker was paid a wage for his work, and kept all that wage. Moreover, the wage was not set by the employer but by the forces of the marketplace, where workers and capitalists met as legal equals, each side entitled to seize whatever penny of advantage it could.

What was then the source of rents and profits? As we already know, Smith saw it in a fundamental inequality of bargaining strengths that prevented labor's wages from absorbing the full value of the product. "A landlord, a farmer, a master manufacturer, or a merchant," he wrote, "though they did not employ a single workman, could generally live a year or two upon the stock [capital] which they had already acquired. Many workmen could not subsist a week, few could subsist a month, and scarce any a year without employment."[9] Thus the "necessity" of employment, despite the contractual freedom that set it so decisively apart from the status of serf or slave, provided the disparity in social power from which arose the rights to payment called *rent,* or to claims to a residual called *profit,* without which the access to resources called *employment* would not be offered.

Were these rent and profit "deductions" (as Smith called them)[10] a new form of exploitation? Here the matter became more difficult to analyze. There was never the slightest doubt as to the exploitative character of the wealth that appeared as pyramids and temple complexes, wrung from forced labor and devoted to the glory of Olympian rulers. But what of the factories and mills that were the great works of capitalism? However skewed the

9. Smith, *Wealth,* p. 66.

10. Ibid., p. 65.

bargaining arrangement, the labor that built those edifices of capital was freely hired and could freely quit. And whatever profits the mills and factories earned, their justification was not the vainglory of their owners but the creation of flows of commodities, more and more of which were destined for consumption by the working classes themselves.

Was this still exploitation? No such idea appears in Smith, despite his use of the word *deductions.* In Marx, as we know, the theme of exploitation is central, based at bottom on an analysis of social relationships not so different from Smith's unequal bargaining strengths. What is different is that Marx sees capitalism as possessing a remarkable capacity to conceal the exploitative nature of its gains by the fiction of an active "Monsieur le Capital" and "Madame la Terre" who make contributions to, not exactions from, the total product. As for modern economists, the issue has largely been forgotten. The substitution of pyramids of commodities for pyramids of stone has pushed the issue out of consciousness and perhaps conscience. This is not surprising in light of what capitalism has brought: in 1750 the level of material well-being in Europe was roughly equal to that of the parts of the world we today call underdeveloped. By 1930 the level was four times higher; today it is seven times higher.[11]

V

Thus we begin to see that capitalism is the source of fundamental changes in the act of work, nowhere clearer

---

11. See above, page 54, note 9.

than in an aspect we have previously ignored. This is the motivation that provided candidates for work—the reasons that men and women agreed to relinquish some portion of their product in order to gain access to resources.

There is no difficulty in explaining this motivation in the first centralized regimes. The recruiting agents were hunger and fear. Men and women acquiesced in submissive arrangements for survival's sake or because military and civil power made it impossible not to do so. In the early days of capitalism, the coming of contractual freedom effectively removed the stimulus of fear but not that of hunger. Sheer survival remained the principal reason why workers showed up at the hated and feared mills and mines. And even today, when one looks into the reasons why men and women work as migrant pickers, or make the hazardous and anxiety-ridden voyage from their Caribbean lands to the sweatshops of New York, or line up for employment in the factory districts of Hong Kong or Seoul, we are forcibly reminded that the recruitment mechanism of the stomach is still in force.

Nonetheless, I do not think that anyone could claim that hunger is the main factor in marshaling the work forces in Western capitalism today. There is no more incontrovertible evidence for this than that it is possible to live in Western capitalism—and in its more advanced European versions, to live at a decent level—without working. Yet it is the common observation that men and women want work, even when they do not have to have it; that few individuals are happy on welfare; in short, that work is looked on as a desirable condition of life, even though it is no longer essential for life.

What is the source of this remarkable change in attitude? The reason is self-evident: Work has become the avenue to enjoyments that were previously the prerogative only of those who did not work. Smith has something to say about one of these enjoyments. He is speaking about the state of mind of the man who amasses a fortune: "The rich man glories in his riches because he feels they naturally draw upon him the attention of the world . . . and he is fonder of his wealth on this account than for all the other advantages it procures him."[12] Although the riches that capitalism makes available to ordinary people through work may be minuscule compared with those that accrue to property, the kinds of pleasures they afford are measured in the same coin of self-esteem and the approval of the world. The capitalist relationship of free contractual engagement opens the possibility of social advancement to ordinary men, and ordinary men come crowding in to seize the opportunity.

Closely allied with this motive of prestige and social standing is that of power. Capitalism is the first civilization in which the upper class "works" in ways that would have been regarded with disdain by the upper classes of previous social orders. Why do businessmen put in their long, frenetic hours? The answer is that they are seeking the modern form of another age-old desideratum—not the power of the military chief or the political ruler but the kind of power that counts in a world run by transactions

---

12. Adam Smith, *The Theory of Moral Sentiments* (1969), p. 70 (part I, sec. 3, chap. 2).

and business negotiations. "Wealth is power," says Smith, quoting Hobbes.[13]

So it is apparent that men and women work under capitalism for very different reasons than in harsher settings where work was only a burden, never a stepping stone or an adventure. Always excepting the poor and the ragged (which embrace a very large number if we allow our gaze to include those in backward regions who are part of the structure of world capitalism), it is nonetheless incontrovertible that the motive of work for at least the middle and upper income levels of capitalism will bear little resemblance to the motives of the wretches who toiled in the coal mines and cotton mills of Dickensian England and even less to the slaves in the Laurentian silver mines of Greece. The difference is that capitalism has combined prestige and power into a new social value, available to many and tempting to all: the value of success. Prior to capitalism, there was triumph, glory, high rank, wealth—but there was no success. Success is the reward of power and prestige that comes from work.

But this raises a critical question. When the president of a company puts in long hours at his desk in pursuit of success does he not more closely resemble in his motivation a commander poring over his plans than the troops following that commander's orders? Would we call the commander's actions *work?* So, too, should we use the word *work* to describe the executive's underlings—and their underlings' underlings—pursuing success as they

---

13. Smith, *Wealth,* p. 31.

waltz their customers around, buck for promotion, or work up their expense accounts? Is the assembly line operative "working" as he does his stint, motivated by dreams of the car he intends to buy? Is a college student working as he cracks his books? A scientist as he adjusts his equipment?

We call all these activities *work* in the same undifferentiated way that we use the term to describe the Kalahari hunter. But the whole thrust of our argument is that the blanket use of the word disguises the quintessential aspect that separates true work from other kinds of tasks and activities. The difference, if I may express it once again, is that *work* refers to activities undertaken in a social condition of submission—a condition that results from the inability of individuals to avail themselves directly of the resources they need. That critical distinction must now be tested against the conditions of modern capitalist life. When success becomes a chief motivation, when striving and ambition rather than abject necessity emerge as the driving forces in society, can we still maintain that work contains a central core of subordination?

VI

The answer is certainly not a simple one. I have sufficiently stressed the freedom-related aspects of work that play so vital a role in changing the motivation of the population. Now we must look again at the other side of the coin, examining the nature of the submission that is also part of the work relationship.

I shall begin by quoting Adam Smith once more. He is speaking of the organization of work in a pin factory, the paradigmatic work-institution of the capitalist mode of production. What he notes is that labor has become a process that can be broken down into discrete operations performed by different individuals. "One man draws out the wire, another straights it, a third cuts it, a fourth points it. . . ." Thus Smith explains the famous principle of the divisions of labor whose consequence is that ten persons who, working separately could not perhaps make a single pin each, together make forty-eight thousand of them.[14]

The subordination here is obvious. It lies in a relinquishing of control over one's work life, a surrender of the autonomy of the body and mind to a pace and to movements designed by another. Nothing like this previously existed in the centralized modes of production where, however crushing the task, its form and basic rhythm remained within the control of the worker. Under capitalism the division of labor reduces the activity of labor to dismembered gestures. The consequence, of course, is the vast multiplication of output that is capitalism's gift to civilization, but the multiplication, it must not be forgotten, results from the power of property to exact its submissive price. Smith himself was uneasy about that price: "The man whose whole life is spent in performing a few simple operations . . . ," he wrote, "has no occasion to exercise his understanding . . . and generally becomes as stupid and ignorant as it is possible for a human creature to become."[15]

---

14. Ibid., pp. 4, 5.
15. Ibid., p. 734.

We need not, however, look for submission only in the extreme case of the assembly line worker. Subordination is also present in the normal, everyday, rarely questioned fact of hierarchical management itself, in the fact that work consists of production carried out in a military-like fashion. In this arrangement, the officers are the representatives of capital, just as in previous modes of production they were representatives of imperial and other rule. Once again, however, the subordinative element is veiled. The rights of the owners of equipment to "give" employment and as a consequence to establish the basic lines of authority over work—determining the boundaries of jobs, the allowable reach of each individual's autonomy—are so much a part of daily existence that it scarcely occurs to us that freedom and subordination are integrally involved.

The subordinative aspect of work is further veiled because it is only incidentally located in the person of a particular employer. There are tyrannical bosses, of course—the mainstay of the gossip of work. But no matter how tyrannical, a boss cannot maintain his power over a worker who exercises his or her legal right to quit. It is not so simple—indeed, it is impossible—to escape the tyranny of the system to which all are exposed, including the boss. That tyranny is exerted through the workings of the marketplace, more inscrutable than those of a fabled Oriental despot, more deaf to pleas for mercy than the most bored seneschal, more difficult to direct or change (some economists tell us nowadays) than the stubbornest autocrat.

So there remains a core of submission in the act of work in capitalism, for all its attendant motives of ambition and achievement and despite its remarkable advances in contractual liberty. This is the aspect of the system noted by Marx and Engels when they wrote in *The German Ideology* that "in imagination individuals seem freer under the dominance of the bourgeoisie than before, because their conditions of life seem more accidental; in reality, of course, they are less free because they are more subjected to the violence of things."[16]

I am not sure how many serfs or slaves would lend their assent to Marx's and Engels's cavalier "of course," but we can nonetheless see what they mean. Work under capitalism does not require bowing one's head to a lord or master—not beyond the point of endurance at any rate—but it does require bowing one's head to the violence of things. Work appears or disappears under capitalism by the ebb and flow of economic forces as invisible but as powerful as hurricane winds. Work for the individual is immeasurably freer than it was in the past, but for the collectivity of individuals it is not. The submission to the dictates of the system itself is not as overt or dramatic as that required on a field of combat or before a court of law, but it is there just the same—all the more overmastering because it seems no more than the warp and woof of daily life.

VII

Yet, to turn the coin over one more time, freedom is also present under capitalism, however incomplete or partial; and a taste of freedom whets the appetite for more. The sense of personal fulfillment and psychological expansion that work brings when it leads to success; the self-esteem

---

16. Karl Marx and Friedrich Engels, *The German Ideology* (1947), p. 77.

that floods our being when we have done our assigned tasks well, even if they bring no particular distinction; the bond to social reality that Freud believed to be the redeeming aspect of work—all these lead ineluctably to a desire for the enlargement of that which is invigorating and emancipating in work and the contraction of that which is cramping and submissive, until finally we arrive—at a higher level, of course—back to the blissful state of primitive society where men and women carry on the activities that sustain their material lives with no greater sense of subordination than when they fulfill its nurtural or cultural requirements. In a word, we glimpse the tantalizing vision of a world without work.

Is such a world possible? Let me begin with a necessary qualification. The vision of a world without work is not to be interpreted as a world without effort, perhaps exhausting effort, or a world without personal achievement (and, of course, the risk of personal failure). At least for us success-inoculated Westerners, such an existence would be, in Hannah Arendt's words, a "lifeless life."[17] But indolence is not at all the quality we seek in a world without work. What is at stake is not a society without striving and effort but a society without submissive striving, without subordinative effort.

That makes the issue sharper. Two general vistas now appear. The first, and the most generally considered, is technological. Can we create a world in which submissive effort will become unnecessary because machines will take over all tasks? If we have Aristotle's lyre that plucks itself

17. Arendt, *The Human Condition*, p. 120.

and his loom that weaves by itself generalized into robots that raise our food, mine our ores, perform all or nearly all our factory and office tasks, would we not then be free to consume their output, much as the hunters and gatherers consume the output of nature?

Such a robotic mode of production now seems technically imaginable, if we look far enough ahead—a partially robotized world is already near enough to raise disturbing questions with respect to the possibilities for employment. A fully robotized world would indeed be one in which there would be no need for men and women to submit to the relationship of subordination, because machines would perform their tasks, yielding up all their returns. What sort of world would such a regime of machinery be? The prospect is disconcerting and unnerving. I will venture only one speculation with regard to it. Surely the emplacement of such a robotic mode would render the present social order as obsolete as the emplacement of centralized power rendered obsolete the domestic mode. It would be the end of capitalism, the beginning of we know not what.

The second vista is more attractive. It asks us to imagine whether our existing system could not gradually expand its prestige and power-oriented jobs until virtually all work was conducted under the aegis of ambition, not duress, so that subordination and submission would simply disappear.

I have no doubt that a great many constraints that now encumber work—especially in its sapping division of labor and its hierarchical disposition of jobs—can be lessened. Indeed, such a freeing of work may well become a central item on the agenda of liberal capitalism or democratic socialism in our time. But this loosening of the constraints on work is still very far from the achievement of a social order without subordination and submission. Modern material life is intricately interdependent and ecologically and technically dangerous. The activities of men and women, interacting with complex machinery and vast bottled-up energy, is completely different from the activities of men and women roaming the forests or the grasslands for game or berries. Every act of production in modern society generates repercussions, some of them tidal in magnitude. Thus the activities of modern society must be carried out under some regulating and disciplining oversight, be it the Market, Planning, or some combination of these. Because that is the case, work—and I now stress to the utmost its inner core of submission to social direction—is essential to maintain civilization as we know it. A world without work is a fantasy, and a dangerous fantasy at that.

Yet that is not quite the end of the matter. Some form of supervision is unavoidable in a technologically interlinked and technically dangerous world. But the question is what sort of supervision that might be. In the past, the directing, order-bestowing force has been that of domination—the largely unchallengeable hegemony of small groups whose objectives and values determined the manner in which the great mass of humanity would find access to livelihood. That describes the nakedly exploitative character of the civilizations of the ancient Chinese and Aztecs and Egyptians and Europeans. It still applies to much of the civilization of modern times.

Must this condition of domination continue? Or is it possible that the submission and discipline of work might become the free act of obedience of all members of society to their own purposes, not to those of a small minority? Can work, the first and perhaps most basic form of social subordination, become the first and perhaps most emancipatory form of social responsibility? Can men and women, by regulating their own relationships and obligations of work, establish a foundation on which will rest a similar self-regulation of other aspects of the human condition?

I do not intend to answer these questions, either in the pious affirmations or the skeptical negatives to which they so easily lead. We will only learn their answers by struggling to achieve whatever freedom is possible within work—not from work. I will content myself by pointing out that these are the immense questions—at once sobering and inspiring—to which any inquiry into the implications and meanings of the act of work must finally come.

5

The Problem of Value*

LIKE THE QUESTION of work, the problem of value is not held in much esteem in contemporary economic thought. The term has acquired an antiquarian cast, conjuring up disputes as remote from current concerns as the *Methodenstreit*—the bitter German dispute over methodology—of a century ago. Indeed, I would venture that most economists today do not even see the need for a "theory" of value, as distinct from a theory of price, and would in fact be hard pressed to explain the difference between the two.

It is, however, this very condition of disesteem and disregard that prompts me to take up an age-old and exhaustively discussed subject once again. For I have gradually become convinced—myself starting from the commonly held position of indifference to and impatience with the matter—that the neglect of value does not remove the issue from economics but only leads to its covert appearance in harmful form; that the questions raised by value are not antiquarian but perennial (and, I should add,

---

*This essay originally appeared in *Social Research,* Summer 1983. The reader is reminded that this is a somewhat technical chapter.

not elementary but elemental); and that varying approaches to value, far from being mere pedagogical devices for periodizing the history of economic thought—classical political economy with its "labor theory" of value, postclassical with its "utility theory"—powerfully influence the constitution of economic thought itself by identifying different elements within the social process as strategic for our understanding of it.

I

For all the debate that has surrounded the problem of value, it remains a difficult—worse, elusive—term to define. As we shall see, the elements within social life that are caught in the meshes of the inquiry into value vary widely from one conception to another. This makes it necessary to begin by posing a key question: Is there a *general problematic of value*—a central issue that can be discerned within the wide spectrum of definitions and conceptions that the subject embraces? I believe there is such a problematic, and it will clarify my purpose if I set it forth with no further ado.

The general problematic of value, as I see it, is the effort to tie the surface phenomena of economic life to some inner structure or order. This problematic arises because economics is unavoidably involved in two intimately related but essentially distinct tasks. One of these is the investigation of various empirical aspects of the process of social provisioning, the great objective of economic scrutiny. This task of economics usually, although not always, concentrates on the prices, and to a lesser degree the quantities, of goods that emerge into the sphere of social circulation and exchange. Here is where we find such examples of economic inquiry as the analysis of problems of supply and demand, the specification of an econometric model of the cycle, the construction of an input-output matrix, and the like.

Empirical investigation into the provisioning process is an essential, indeed a constitutive, part of economic inquiry, but it is not the only such part. Equally necessary for the existence of what we call economic thought is a level of abstract inquiry—an inquiry directed not at the "facts" of economic life but at some structure or principle "behind" the facts. In this second of its tasks, economics deals with empirical data only as indications—necessarily incomplete and very often misleading—with respect to the object of its investigation. It looks beyond appearances for essences, as Marx would say; or beyond the data for covering laws, in the positivist vocabulary. Economics now becomes an inquiry into the systemic properties, the structural attributes, the tendencies and sometimes even the *telos* of the provisioning process. Thus behind empirical investigations into allocation problems we have theoretical premises as to the "workings" of the price mechanism; behind the functional equations of econometric models there are assumptions as to the "laws" of behavior of individuals, or perhaps even the "laws of motion" of the capitalist system; behind input-output matrices are "production functions," equally abstract representations of the idealized behavior of the industries in question.

The value problematic concerns the nature of this "deep structure" within economic life and the manner in which it influences the surface phenomena of production and distribution. It must therefore be apparent why the search for such a structure, the explanation of its configuration, and its connection with the world of appearances is a perennial question of elemental importance. Value theory (the "theory" is a redundancy in that the task is inherently theoretical) is the name we attach to the search for processes or structures that impart orderly configurations to the empirical world, akin to the arcs created in iron filings under the influence of a magnet.

The magnetic field that is the objective of the value problematic also explains why value is usually so entwined with prices rather than with other elements of the empirical world, such as the quality of working life or the composition of output or consumption. The answer is that prices are the means by which market societies in general, and capitalist societies in particular, establish social coherence from the otherwise uncoordinated activities of their actors. Prices link the world of action and that of order. Value "theory" is therefore indispensable for understanding how the capitalist system, largely guided by price stimuli, tends toward some kind of determinate outcome.

It should be noted that value inquiry is not specifically interested in the *mechanisms* by which the inner principles impart their structure to the outer surface. These mechanisms are largely the maximizing drive and the competitive pressure of a market order. Much hinges on how these drives and pressures are described (short- or long-run maximizing; disciplinary or destructive competition), but in all cases the mechanisms only serve as the means by which the empirical world is guided toward a certain configuration. The search for value is an inquiry into the rationale and characteristics of that configuration. As Adolph Lowe puts it: "Suppose that a universal amnesia were to wipe out the knowledge of all present prices, would there be a rule for reestablishing them?"[1]

II

Some conception of value—some idea of a structure or order behind the flux of activity—is therefore integral to economic thought, for economic thought is an effort to *explain* the nature of the phenomenal world. What is surprising is that, after so many decades of discussion and debate, the nature of that order-bestowing substance or process remains unresolved. Therefore, in taking up the attempts to unravel the puzzle in rough chronological order of origin, I wish to do more than rehearse the well-known—and some not-so-well-known—difficulties of these approaches; I want to tease out from their very incompletion some clues as to the constitution of economic thought itself.

There have been five distinct attempts to unravel the value problematic. The oldest candidate for the task seems at first to lie outside the scope of economic inquiry. This is the *normative* determination of standards of price or of other economic activities. The term normative essentially connotes some moral (and of course political) resolution to the search for order-bestowing principles. As such, the normative approach establishes the order, or lack of order, of an existing configuration of prices or other empirical

1. Adolph Lowe, "Is Economic Value Still a Problem?," *Social Research* (Winter 1981), p. 789.

elements by its conformity with a socially determined standard.

Many standards have served this parametric function: commutative justice for Aristotle; "just prices" (absence of usurious or other improper mercantile practices) for Aquinas and the medieval schoolmen; a system of remuneration devoid of "exploitation" for J. B. Clark; welfare maximization of consumers for Pareto; goal-adequate systemic adjustments for Lowe; and yet others.[2] What is identificatory about these social norms is that they posit ideal configurations that will not be attained in the absence of moral or political action. All require that society's arrangements be altered, whether by fiat or by some degree of intervention into market outcomes.

As with all value-resolving efforts, the normative approach has strengths and weaknesses. The strengths lie in the direct center placement and open recognition of an element of *valuation* that is a haunting but unacknowledged presence in all conceptions of value. The etymological significance of the word reveals what all the protestations in favor of "value-free" (more properly, valuation-free) inquiry will not remove, namely, the inextricable presence of a concern for a structure of economic order that is deemed "good" as well as merely functional. The fact that we rule out of consideration all "orderly" solutions to economic problems that involve terms such as zero employment or zero output suffices to demonstrate

2. Aristotle, *Politics,* bk. 1, and *Nicomachean Ethics,* bk. 5; Aquinas, *Summa Theologica,* q. 77; J. B. Clark, *The Distribution of Wealth* (1899); Vilfredo Pareto, *Manual of Political Economy* (1971); Lowe, *On Economic Knowledge*, pt. 4.

that the search for a principle of value requires socially acceptable as well as technically sufficient determinations. Many commentators have recognized the validity of this concern, Schumpeter, for instance, stating that "[p]reoccupation with the ethics of pricing . . . is precisely one of the strongest motives a man can have for analyzing actual market mechanisms."[3]

The gravamen of the normative approach is therefore that the order manifested by an economic structure should be that which its ruling element (including, of course, the most broadly defined democratic constituency) desires it to be. But if this is the signal strength of the normative approach, it is also its most evident weakness. Two objections have been lodged against this naked declaration of moral or political priority. The first is the undeniable arbitrariness of political valuation, always open to challenge from a differing political starting point. This argument brings us to the affirmation and defense of moral and political principles in general, a vast subject that can only be recognized, not analyzed, here.[4]

But the second objection is more germane, if less profound. It is the charge that political or moral intervention

---

3. Joseph Schumpeter, *History of Economic Analysis* (1954), p. 60. See also Karl Marx, *Theory of Surplus Value,* Part III (1971), pp. 267–297; and Adolph Lowe, "The Normative Basis of Economic Value," in Sidney Hook, ed., *Human Values and Economic Policy* (1967). See also Lowe, "Is Economic Value Still a Problem?," pp. 813–814.

4. The subject is nothing less than that of justice, with which economics has always had an ambivalent relation. One of the reasons for the impact of John Rawls's *A Theory of Justice* was its explicit attempt to marry ethical considerations with economic techniques, employing the morally neutral means of indifference analysis to build an argument in favor of a morally charged desideratum of income distribution.

will be of no avail because some other ordering principle will assert itself over and against the wishes of the moralists. This charge is frequently brought by proponents of a utility approach to value, who assert, for example, that efforts to establish norms for wages are doomed to failure because "the market" will invalidate these efforts in one way or another. Whether this charge is itself politically motivated is a matter that need not detain us, for the point can also be made that politically or morally determined prices may not be compatible with the *technical* requirements of provisioning—an example amply illustrated by disastrous episodes in the history of many centrally planned socialist economies. This objection thus leads logically to the second of the answers to the value problematic itself—an answer that eschews all reference to moral standards and that seeks the principle of value in some entirely nonmoral element or principle discoverable within the economic world.

III

This approach to value, also vaguely traceable to Aristotle (*Politics,* Book I), resolves the problematic by attributing to "labor" the role of an order-bestowing force. By virtue of its universal presence throughout the world of produced objects, labor imparts varying weights, or quanta, of "value substance" that establish the normal (not normative) price relations among commodities. Here we can do no better than to consider Adam Smith's formulation in chapter 6 of the *Wealth of Nations,* quoted approvingly by Ricardo as a model exposition of the basis for "exchange value"—the abstract element behind price:

In that early and rude state of society which precedes both the accumulation of stock and the appropriation of land, the proportion between the quantities of labour necessary for acquiring different objects seems to be the only circumstance which can afford any rule for exchanging them for one another. If among a nation of hunters, for example, it usually costs twice the labour to kill a beaver which it does to kill a deer, one beaver should naturally exchange for or be worth two deer. It is natural that what is usually the produce of two days' or two hours' labour, should be worth double of what is usually the produce of one day's or one hour's labour.[5]

This classic statement serves our purpose very well, for it explicitly avoids all the problems of departures from labor-determined value arising from profit on capital. The exposition is so simple, so carefully phrased, and so intuitively compelling that it is difficult to think of any other explanation ("rule," says Smith) behind prices in a society where property in land or capital exerts no claim on the product.

In fact, this very intuitive appeal is the source of widespread misunderstanding. For the labor theory in the classical parable does *not* explain why two deer will exchange for one beaver. The seemingly self-evident rule begs questions and assumes premises that are entirely absent from the parable itself. Moreover, it does not explicate what is meant by the "value" of which labor time is presumably the source. Not only is the rule of exchange obscure, but so is the nature of the stuff that is being exchanged.

First the rule. Why must two deer exchange for one

---

5. Smith, *Wealth*, p. 47; David Ricardo, *Principles of Political Economy and Taxation* (1952), p. 13.

beaver, assuming that it takes half as long to kill one deer as one beaver? The exchange rule requires at least two prior conditions for its operation:

(1) Individuals who engage in exchange must wish to (or need to) maximize the "value" of their net receipts. We leave unexamined for the moment the nature of this value, to make the crucial point that without *maximizing behavior* (whether imposed by scarcity or by social conditioning) the exchange ratios need not reflect labor times expended. The technical requirements of social reproduction may set limits to these ratios, but these need not be the equalizing rates implied by Smith's model. In a word, a society may operate at less than its most efficient trading ratios. Moreover it *will* operate at these less-than-most efficient ratios if any of the trading partners is not a maximizer. In a word, Smith's parable assumes that a full-fledged market society, with all its institutional and cultural underpinnings, will be the milieu in which the deer hunter and the beaver hunter meet to do business.

(2) The deer–beaver exchange rate also assumes a prevailing *disutility of labor.* If hunting is experienced as a positive pleasure—a net utility—there is no reason why the trophies should exchange on any basis other than their idiosyncratic use values. The assumption that they will exchange on the basis of expended labor times requires the necessary condition that labor is experienced as an onerous task, a condition that may be historically valid but that is not explicit in the parable.

These difficulties already make it clear that the classical paradigm of the beaver and the deer fails to accomplish its purpose of explaining why objects exchange at their observed prices, for reasons other than obedience to social norms. This is true even before the complicating elements of capital, or the complex procedures of a "market society" are introduced into the picture. But there is an even more fundamental theoretical objection to be lodged. It concerns the nature of the "labor" that creates "exchange value"—the structure that governs actual prices. The quotation marks call to our attention that both terms conceal problems of which Smith, Ricardo, and the other classical writers were completely unaware.

The problem concerns the nature of labor itself and the manner in which it can endow an object with properties that will bring it within the ambit of some regulatory influence. Labor unquestionably endows objects with one common element that might serve as the gateway to such an ordering influence, in that it is labor that moves things from the natural to the social world. In the natural world things have uses (the term "use values" is a question-begging phrase), but these useful things are without prices and therefore outside the reach of any ordering influence until they have been appropriated, or moved into the social world. But even after appropriation, there is no basis for systematic pricing other than the adventitious circumstances of relative scarcity and utility, in which labor plays no role. Ricardo is entirely correct in excluding scarce and rare (nonreproducible) objects from his "labor theory of value."

The act of moving objects from their natural into a social state is, however, only the most general socializing function of labor. The more specific and important function involves production, where more or less determinate processes of labor regularly convert objects of nature into objects of social importance. If these objects are thereupon to be priced according to their labor "substance" it becomes necessary to understand what that substance consists of and how it is measured. Here is where the classical theory fails at a conceptual level. For labor does not impart a "substance" to commodities in any physical sense. The energies and intelligence that Smith's workman exerts when he "straights" the pins in a pin factory or that Ricardo's hunter displays in stalking his deer do not enter their products. In both cases, the effect of labor is to alter the physical attributes, and thereby the usefulness, of the objects to which it is directed, but that effect does not bestow quanta of "labor stuff" in the manner that a fire bestows quanta of heat on the objects it warms. This statement sounds self-evident, but is the source of much confusion.

How, then, can the classical labor theory of value assert that an hour of labor directed to deer hunting exerts the same influence—that is, will be manifested in the same price—as an hour spent straightening pins? The answer is that it cannot. The argument carries the day by the force of its intuitive appeal and imagery, not by the cogency of its logic. On close inspection there is nothing commensurable in an hour of hunting and an hour of hammering, and there is, therefore, no common quantum of labor energy or input discoverable in each product. Jevons saw this when he wrote that it was "impossible to compare a priori the productive powers of a navvy, a carpenter, an iron-puddler, a schoolmaster, and a barrister." That is why he concluded that the value of labor "must be determined by the value of the product, not the value of the product by the value of labor."[6]

IV

The unsatisfactory nature of the classical resolution leads in several directions. It opens the way for a further examination of Jevons's inversion of the problem. It serves as an appropriate jumping-off point for an examination of Marxian value theory. Or it becomes the proper place to introduce the emendations proposed by Smith and Ricardo, which lead to a quite separate approach to value, a cost-of-production theory.

Because it best accords with the chronological development of our theme, I propose that we now pursue the last of these paths. Every economist knows that Smith, despite his beaver and deer parable, felt impelled to explain prices on a basis different from pure labor inputs. This was because he recognized that, in all social stages beyond that of "rude" society, capital and land were undeniably involved in the pricing process, and that a theory of value that ignored them could not serve as a foundation for explaining the basis of exchange. Thus Smith took his well-known recourse to the description of exchange value as composed of the "natural" prices of the three constituent cost-elements in commodities—the wages of labor, the rent of land, and the profits of capital.[7]

---

6. W. S. Jevons, *The Theory of Political Economy* (1970), p. 187. I have reversed the order of the sentences better to fit into my sequence of thought. The second sentence in the quotation is in italics in the original.

7. Smith, *Wealth,* ch. 6. See also the commentaries by Maurice Dobb, *Theories of Value and Distribution* (1973), and Ronald L. Meek, *Studies in the Labour Theory of Value* (1956).

Every economist also knows that on two counts this is an unsatisfactory basis for resolving the value issue. First, it ignores the fact that wages, rents, and profits are themselves prices whose relation to some ordering principle must be explained rather than passed over. Second, it is mute in the face of the query, "What is the *substance* or, if you will, the *nature* of the 'value' that enters into all three elements?" With respect to labor, as we have seen, the classical economists overlooked the problem of defining a common unit of effort. But even assuming that one could constitute such a unit from labor's "toil and trouble," no counterpart in terms of a basic unit of input was ever adduced for land or capital.*

Thus the cost-of-production value structure cannot be reduced to any foundation other than the "normal" wages, rents, and profits that make up the costs of producing various commodities. As a consequence there is a considerable range of such value structures, depending on various historical circumstances that have produced various "normal" levels of wages and profits. This is not a fatal objection to cost of production as a source of order beneath the price phenomena of society, but it certainly eliminates any suggestion that this order reflects the presence of some kind of universal, objectively determined value substance. Smith's pursuit of value therefore terminates in nothing more than a description of the specific order of prices corresponding to a particular social struc-

---

*Abstinence—that is, not consuming—was suggested by John Stuart Mill and a number of other writers as the "contribution" of capital. It is obviously unsatisfactory on a number of counts: *not* consuming can hardly be called an "input"; it is not uniform (like an hour of labor); and the idea is socially absurd.

ture with its legal prerogatives, its legitimated courses of action, and its traditional political and social habits. The bounded dynamics of Smith's conception of capitalist material progress and moral decay, all taking place within an unchanging social framework, unwittingly reflects the profound consequences of this value presupposition.

With Ricardo the matter takes on a much more sophisticated aspect. Ricardo disposes of the problem of the contribution of land by his postulate of marginal zero-rent land; and he is aware, unlike Smith, that the claim of capital to some part of the value (effort) attributable to labor introduces a systematic dysjunction between a value standard based on labor alone and the price structure of the real world. Because he does not argue, as Smith implicitly does, that capital *adds* to labor's contribution, Ricardo is forced to accept his "six or seven percent" as the minimum reservation price demanded by capitalists—a concession that leads him into what Stigler has called the 93 percent labor theory of value.[8]

Despite his insistence, then, that labor alone is the *source* of all value, in conceding to capital a systematic *influence* on price, as irreducible as labor's "toil and trouble," Ricardo also proposes a version of a cost-of-production explanation of value. There is, however, a difference of some importance between Smith and Ricardo. Smith's tacit assumption that all classes contribute to the (undefined) substance of value allows him to build a harmonist view of the larger dynamics of the system. Ricardo's conception, which rests on an antagonistic rather than comple-

8. George J. Stigler, *Essays in the History of Economics* (1965), ch. 6.

mentary approach to capital's influence on value, leads to a much more divisive view of the consequences of social progress. Diminishing returns to agricultural land become of fulcral importance to his schema of distribution because the receivers of rents and profits must contend for shares of diminishing marginal increments of "labor value" to which they cannot themselves directly contribute.

Ricardo's problem prepares the way for Marx, but there is an important matter to be considered first. We have seen that a cost-of-production theory is not a satisfactory candidate for resolving the value question because it is circular in form and because it has no candidate to serve as the general substance or essential nature of value itself. Yet, as I have said, this is not a fatal objection. The purpose of value, I have now undoubtedly repeated too many times, is to provide a means of linking the phenomena of the empirical world, mainly prices, with some principle or structure. The cost-of-production theory rules out any *abstract* order behind prices—any order that reflects some "essence" of the economic world—but it does not rule out the possibility of establishing order on the basis of historical realities. Wages and profits in various forms are subject to inertial tendencies preserved by pecking orders, reference groups, intergenerational transfers of taste and behavior, community sanctions, legal barriers, and the like, all of which create a framework of order sustained by powerful, although often unacknowledged, social processes.[9]

9. For the importance of social processes in maintaining order within a presumably "market directed" society, see Fred Hirsch, *The Social Limits to Growth* (1976), pp. 137–138.

It is possible, therefore, to take refuge from the difficulties inextricably associated with an abstract approach to value through a kind of skeptical empiricism that looks no farther than those social relationships of power, morality, and perhaps even reason as the basis on which social continuity is grounded and persists, sometimes in the face of disturbances that make those of social reform look trifling.

V

And so we come to the famous Marxian theory of value. Marx, too, looks to the act of labor as the fundamental activity that creates orderly relationships of exchange. But the term *labor* is now decisively redefined. For Smith or Ricardo, labor simply connotes all onerous travail. For Marx, the term takes on special significance when that travail is performed under specific historic conditions. These are the conditions—epitomized by, but not exclusively present under, capitalism—in which labor creates objects not for their immediate enjoyment but as "commodities," objects produced in order to realize their exchangeability for money. The category of value therefore presupposes a society in which relationships of organized exchange have been established and in which a basis for regularizing these relationships has therefore become a necessity. This basis is indeed "labor," but only labor expended on the pursuit of exchange value, whether for the immediate producer or for the capitalist who hires producers. Smith's hunters of beaver and deer would not create value, in Marx's eyes, unless they undertook their tasks with exchange—not personal use—in mind.

Labor performed under these circumstances differs from classical labor in a categorical way. Labor now becomes not just a concrete activity, such as hammering or hunting, but also an *abstract* activity. That is, the act of performing labor in order to create exchange value confers on the concrete efforts of workers an additional dimension, completely missing when labor is performed without exchange as its motive. This new dimension is *commensurability,* the possibility of comparing activities that were formerly beyond comparison. It is this abstract property that converts labor as use value into labor as exchange value, establishing the basis for its designation as the commodity called by Marx *labor power.* As is well known, labor power now takes its place as the foundation of Marx's analysis of the origin of profit and as the key element in the laws of motion of the profit-generating system, capitalism.[10]

The notion of abstract labor is therefore the indispensable idea on which Marx's theory of value is based, a point overlooked by, or unknown to, most conventional economists who speak of "Marxian" value theory.[11] The linkage of the concept of value—once again, an ordering presence "behind" the world of prices—to the appearance of the

---

10. The locus classicus for this discussion is in *Capital,* vol. 1, pp. 1 ff. These pages are among the most demanding in social science. I have benefited from a number of commentaries and exegeses, among them: Lucio Colletti, *From Rousseau to Lenin* (1972), pp. 82–87; E. J. Nell, "Value and Capital in Marxian Economics," in Daniel Bell and Irving Kristol, eds., *The Crisis in Economic Theory* (1982); Ian Steedman et al., *The Value Controversy* (1981); and Alfred Sohn-Rethel, *Intellectual and Manual Labor* (1978).

11. Samuelson, for example, writes extensively about Marxian theory but regularly conflates Marxian and classical views on labor. See Paul Samuelson, *Economics,* 10th ed. (1976), pp. 728, 858.

particular conditions under which labor becomes a commodity introduces into Marx's work an intrinsic historical aspect. Further, it gives to Marxian theory a special significance in that value now becomes a category that reveals relations of hierarchy or domination that are masked by the usual vocabulary of economic discourse. For this reason, Marxian theory is not merely a search for the principle of "horizontal" order—an explanation of the ratios of exchange in the marketplace—but also a key to "vertical" order—the mutual relations of social classes. Here it both resembles and departs from classical cost-of-production theory, also a class analysis. The difference, of course, lies in Marx's unique penetration into the "fetishism" that obscures the meaning of the classical triad of land, labor, and capital. It is this penetration that accounts for the charged role that "the labor theory of value" plays in Marxian analysis and that is indispensable for the "socioanalysis" that is the enduring achievement of this analysis.[12]

At a different level, however, there remains the question as to whether the Marxian theory is a satisfactory means of establishing the horizontal order manifested through prices. This has been the traditional debating ground for

12. A considerable controversy now rages among Marxian economists as to whether the labor theory of value has become excess baggage. See especially Ian Steedman, *Marx after Sraffa* (1977), and Steedman et al., *The Value Controversy.* The argument revolves around conflicting explanations of surplus, one deriving from Marxian exploitation, which involves Marx's labor theory of value, the other from the relationships of a Sraffian model. The Sraffa model seems to me to leave the origin of profit unexplained, much as the Quesnay model, to which it bears a family resemblance, leaves unexplained the origin of the *produit net.*

Marxian value theory, beginning with Böhm-Bawerk and continuing to the present day. At stake here are two principal questions. The first concerns the now infamous transformation problem, namely, the possibility of moving from the realm of value—allocations of socially necessary abstract labor—to that of prices. Since Böhm-Bawerk's time, critics have rejected Marx's solution, at first simply as erroneous, later as incomplete or inadequate. The literature is too vast to be dealt with here, but a summary remark may make it possible to proceed. It is that *all* theoretical approaches to value have difficulty in systematically allowing for the influence on the price structure exerted by the claims of capital. The difficulty does not lie in capital as the embodiment of past labor but in capital as an active social presence exercising a current claim on output—namely, profit. This is the source of Ricardo's perplexity, of the Austrian maze of roundaboutness, and of the difficulties of modern productivity theory with the complex issues raised in the Cambridge controversy.[13]

At this level, the transformation problem is essentially an exercise in logic designed to test whether unpassable gaps lie in the conceptual chain between the magnitudes of measurable value and those of actual prices. The various procedures for overcoming these gaps are enormously involved (although no more than those employed to overcome the problems of a consistent utility theory). The

---

13. For a review of the Böhm-Bawerkian attack, see Roman Rosdolsky, *The Making of Marx's Capital* (1977); for the Cambridge controversy, see G. C. Harcourt, *Some Cambridge Controversies in the Theory of Capital* (1972).

problem is still not settled and set aside, but I think it is fair to state that since Sraffa it is no longer regarded as an inherently unbridgeable caesura in the Marxian argument.[14]

As interest in the transformation problem has lost its sense of crucial significance, another ancient problem has come to the fore—that of the value differentials of different abstract labors. Smith, Ricardo, and Marx agree that different kinds of labor bestow different quanta of value, but they do not make clear the manner in which these differences are determined. In Smith they are settled by the "higgling and bargaining of the market"; in Ricardo by the varying "esteem" attached by the market to different intensities and skills of labor; and in Marx to a "social process that goes on behind the backs of producers." These are not satisfactory answers. By appealing to the market, Smith and Ricardo smuggle in the very elements that their search for an objective determinant of value seeks to exclude, namely, the utility calculus of the marketplace, or the accidents of history. With Marx the establishment of value differentials is regarded as a matter to be addressed at a different level of abstraction from that of *Capital,* but he never got around to writing the book on wage labor in which he intended to explicate the problem, and the matter remains unsatisfactorily dangling.[15]

---

14. The decisive paper is perhaps R. L. Meek's "Mr. Sraffa's Rehabilitation of Classical Economics," reprinted in his *Economics and Ideology* (1967). Recent resolutions include A. Shaikh, "Marx's Theory of Value and the 'Transformation Problem,' " in Jesse G. Schwartz, ed., *The Subtle Anatomy of Capitalism* (1977).

15. Smith, *Wealth,* p. 31; Ricardo, *Principles,* p. 20; Marx, *Capital,* vol. 1 (1977), p. 135. See also Rosdolsky, *Making of Marx's Capital,* ch. 31.

The difficulty here is the confusion engendered by abstract labor compared with concrete labor. There is indeed no elemental unit of concrete labor, and by extension it is impossible to "reduce" concrete labors—skilled, unskilled, trained, untrained—to any common base.[16] This second "transformation problem"—the transformation from concrete to abstract labor—remains as elusive, or nowadays more elusive, than the original transformation problem. The difficulty is that there is no clear explanation of the way in which abstract labor is added (or compounded?) to provide the basis for wage differentials. Certainly the task cannot be referred to the ministrations of the market without introducing the circularity that vitiates Smith's attempts at solution. Granting to Marx that abstract, not concrete, labor is the substance—the essential constitutive element—of value, what determines its magnitude? To my knowledge the question is unanswered, although I have not been convinced that it is unanswerable.

VI

The difficulties of the Marxian approach turn us in the direction in which the history of thought has also turned.

---

16. Lowe, "Is Economic Value Still a Problem?," p. 808. There is an issue here worth a brief detour involving the terminology with which we discuss different qualities of labor. For every kind of task there exists a gradient of differences among its performers. The differences may be attributed to "innate" talent, to dexterity or experience, or to training. We tend to speak of trained labor as "skilled," an appellation that blurs the important contribution of talent or experience. In actual life we find skilled "unskilled" labor—e.g., dexterous janitors—and unskilled "skilled" labor—e.g., clumsy surgeons. I raise this issue because we easily confuse the quite separate bases on which labor differentials may be based or justified.

The originators of postclassical utility theory were undoubtedly seeking a less "subversive" approach to value than the labor theory as they understood it (justifying labor's "right" to the entire product),[17] but they were undoubtedly driven as well by a genuine desire to find an ordering principle that would circumvent the problems that Jevons described. In particular they sought, and believed they had found, an answer to the value problematic that had occurred to everyone since Aristotle—to wit, grounding the order-bestowing principle behind price in use values rather than in labor embodiments.

This achieved three purposes. First, it established a relation between price and usefulness that had seemed bafflingly absent to earlier investigators—the water and diamond paradox of ancient lineage. Second, it extended the explanatory reach of the value principle from the limited range of price phenomena to the wider area of prices and *quantities,* a hitherto unexplained but certainly important element in the world of empirical realities for which underlying principles were to be discovered. And third, it encompassed a range of price phenomena that had formerly escaped systematic explication—namely, the market prices of nonreproducible goods, or simply the aberrations from normal price, that had hitherto been relegated to "supply and demand" without further analysis.

The postclassicists, from the obscure Gossen to the commanding person of Marshall, accomplished this feat

---

17. For a discussion of the subversive threat of the "labor theory" of value, see Guy Routh, *The Origin of Economic Ideas* (1975) and Meek, *Economics and Ideology.*

by shifting the ground in a crucially important way. The classical and preclassical economists had considered use values as *objective* characteristics of commodities—the tensile strength of steel, the pliability of cotton—for which indeed no common substance of value could be discovered and no rule of value magnitude prescribed. The postclassicists shifted attention to the *subjective* properties of these selfsame objective characteristics, fastening on the varying "utilities" that could be derived from any fixed set of use values. From this arose first the idea of cardinal, then ordinal, preference rankings, the bedrock on which a systematic approach to supply and demand could be grounded.

The achievements and usefulness of utility theory, usually referred to as "price theory," are today so much a part of the stock in trade of economics that I may be spared a further exposition of its strengths. Let me concentrate instead on its weaknesses as a resolution of the value problem. They are essentially three and, although familiar, bear repetition.

The first may be called the operational difficulty of the utility approach. This weakness, recognized originally by Edgeworth and Walras, concerns the extreme assumptions required to reach a determinate equilibrium from the starting point of the exercise. Effectively, the postulation of a general equilibrium begs the serious, perhaps unsolvable, question of how a universe of participants will move toward such a resting point.

The second difficulty is of a conceptual kind. It raises the question of whether a constellation of monads, of whom nothing is known but their utility maps and their maximizing propensities, is sufficient to specify a general equilibrium. This conceptual problem itself breaks into two. One aspect, stressed by Hahn, raises the hurdle of the illimitable numbers of intercommodity and intertemporal orderings that must be known for such an equilibrium to be imaginable. The Arrow-Debreu formulation fails to deal with the need to enumerate all such contingent markets—for example, the preference map for umbrellas next Tuesday. Without such a complete enumeration, the general equilibrium specification cannot be complete, and there can be no assurance that even minute omissions may not give rise to considerable variations in the overall ordering.[18]

The other conceptual knot involves the circularity of the utility approach. The array of prices and quantities that emerges from the interaction of monads arises from the tastes and capacities of the actors. These in turn reflect their initial endowments of income and preference. Circularity enters insofar as the division of income into wages and profits, which certainly shapes the propensities of the actors, is itself the consequence of the functional division of income in the preceding period. This endless regress deprives the array of simultaneous equations of the very thing needed to establish order—namely, a knowable, objective starting point or premise.[19]

Third, the utility approach excludes from its order-

---

18. See Frank Hahn's review of the general problem in *Public Interest*, Special Issue, 1980, p. 132, and in *Lloyd's Bank Review*, June 1982.

19. Lowe, "Is Economic Value Still a Problem?," pp. 796–797.

bestowing reach the activity of producers, who are motivated by profits rather than the satisfactions of consumption. It thereby leaves out of account the demand side of the wage bargain and confines its analytic powers to the explication of consumer demand and direct labor supply.

For these and still other reasons, one might ask why such a clearly inadequate approach to value commands such near-unanimous support among contemporary economists. I think the answers are two. First, very few economists actually use utility analysis as a serious means of resolving the value problematic. When the point at issue is the order-bestowing properties of the market system, a cost-of-production approach is regularly employed in which prices are explained as the sum of *institutionally determined* flows of wages, rents, and profits with suitable allowances for economies of scale and other technological considerations. It is especially striking in this regard that economists regularly resort to a cost-of-production approach when compiling data for gross national product or when comparing the products of two or more years. From a view that sees utilities as the fundamental and irreducible building blocks of price, gross national product is a meaningless concept, the "summation" of individual experiences of pleasure and pain. This has no more validity than the summation of the enjoyments of an audience at a concert.[20]

Second, I suspect that the utility approach to price

20. It is noteworthy that Keynes used a "labor unit" to ground *The General Theory* on a basis that permitted aggregation. Macro theory requires such an objective concept of wealth, which utility theory cannot provide.

(with the unconscious substitution of a more manageable cost-of-production approach wherever needed) recommends itself because it avoids troublesome considerations of class conflict and cooperation as the fundamental problem of social order, and puts in their place a view of social order as the outcome of individuals contending for pleasure or avoiding pain in an environment of scarcity. Whatever violence this may do to history—and I believe it is a fictive account at the level of Locke's social contract—it is much in tune with the conservative ideology of our time, and indeed helps to create and support that ideology.

VII

Incomplete though they are, these comments should suffice to indicate that utility theory also fails to cut the Gordian knot of the value problematic. Thus I suggest it is now time to reflect back over the value problem and to inquire why so many efforts have failed to come to a wholly satisfactory conclusion.

Let me pose the issue a final time. Is there an underlying order that asserts itself in the flux of economic events, as do magnetic fields of force on the disposition of iron filings? Pursuing the metaphor, what is the nature of these force fields, and why do the particles respond to their order-bestowing influence?

The latter question throws some light over the complex issue. Magnetic fields do not affect particles of sand, and the ordering principles of value will not affect all social particles alike. In particular, only those social particles that have been conditioned by historic experience to seek maximizing objectives and to engage in competitive behavior will become subject to the order-bestowing influences of abstract labor or utility. This excludes from the reach of value theory based on these fundamental principles all homeostatic, traditional, premarket, and specifically precapitalist societies and, to an increasing degree, "postcapitalist" societies as well. It is to these systems that normative or historical resolutions apply with special pertinence, although the preservation of a realm of "noneconomic" behavior even in the most market-oriented systems, and the possible presence of some degree of maximizing behavior even in the most "nonmarket" societies, suggests the need to seek explanations based on norms and inertial patterns even in capitalism and to look for evidences of a labor- or utility-based order even in primitive systems or under socialist regimes.

Therefore part of the unsatisfactory resolution of the problem lies simply in the historical nature of economic society itself, which changes its principle of magnetism under different social dispensations. But the matter can be pushed one step beyond that. Economists are interested primarily in the order-bestowing principles in societies that have succumbed to the magnetic force of maximization and in which we have all become iron filings in the guise of socialized "economic beings." It is in these societies primarily that the value problematic takes on its mysterious properties, in which the "deep structure" of order seems to lodge in the systematic influence of forces more abstract than the normative strivings of ruling orders or the silent workings of the microprocesses of tradition and culture. Here I believe that only one candidate for such a definitive principle has not been ruled out, namely, the quanta of abstract labor, suitably weighted by some as yet inadequately explained calculus which would serve as a starting point from which the real-world configuration of prices could be explained.

I do not know whether such a successful effort to establish an abstract labor basis for value could be achieved. Nothing like the effort to explain and rescue utility theory as a basis for value has yet been devoted to the explication of an abstract labor theory. One reason for this is undoubtedly the misgivings with which conventional economists are likely to view the concept of abstract labor itself, half empirical, half metaphysical, and very much out of tune with the prevailing positivist approach to social reality. Yet equally strange concepts underlie all fields of inquiry—mass and force in physics, intention and intellection in psychology, universal and particular in philosophy. The idea of abstract labor admittedly takes us beyond the boundary lines of a conventional positivist approach to social reality, but that is certainly no reason not to pursue the track as far as it can be followed.

Perhaps of greater importance in explaining the reluctance of conventional economics seriously to consider abstract labor as a possible foundation for the value problematic is a wariness of the larger implications of a Marxian analysis. This wariness in turn is based to a large degree on a distaste for the philosophical determinism and political bias to which Marxian analysis is susceptible. Without wishing to exonerate much Marxian analysis of the tendency to portray as "inevitable" that which is merely desired, I would call attention to the implacable determinism of modern price theory, based on formal axiomatics, and remind my readers that the serving up of normative goals disguised as positive statements is an ancient failing of all social science for which no remedy has yet been found.

6

Adam Smith's Capitalism*

THESE LAST CHAPTERS explore visions and ideologies, words whose meanings we will examine in due course. The place to begin, of course, is with Adam Smith. An image floats before Smith's eyes—an image of a society that is integrally connected with, although it is by no means a likeness of, our own. Our immediate interest in Smith is to discover how that image was conceived, what elements of the existing social scene it incorporated, and of course in what ways it failed to foresee developmental tendencies that we consider to be of central importance. Behind that interest, however, lies a larger problem—to make ourselves aware of the degree to which all economic analysis is permeated by, and indeed founded on, such preconscious visions and ideologies.

I

Smith never used the word capitalism, any more than did Marx, but also like Marx his work is a drama of

*Originally published as "The Nature and Logic of Capitalism According to Adam Smith" in *Beschäftigung, Vertailung, and Konjunctur: Festschrift für Adolph Lowe,* Universität Bremen, Bremen, 1984.

"capitals"—the complex movements and interactions brought about by the generalized expansion and mutual encroachments of the enterprises that are the vehicles and vessels of capital. The drama affects most immediately the central theme of the scenario, which is the gathering of additional capital through the social and technical means at hand; but it reaches out, as we shall see, to embroil the general society in structural, ideological, and existential changes that are of primary significance.

What is remarkable about the *Wealth,* as what is also remarkable about *Capital,* is that both books project an inherent logic into an historic, but undated future—not without flaws of omission and commission, but with such fundamental prescience that we recognize the validity of their interior logics all the more for having preceded and anticipated the general direction of what was to come, not merely having explained it after the fact.

Smith described his union as a system of "perfect liberty"—a designation that emphasizes the contractual freedom of wage labor (with its implicit recognition of property rights), as well as institutional elements such as orderly government, a condition of established social relations and the presence of the vital market institutions. But these institutions are themselves built on various psychological "givens" that are the real bedrock of his system.

I shall mention only two of them. The first is the drive that supplies the vital force for the system, namely the desire to "better our condition," that takes the form of a ceaseless need for the accumulation of capital. For Smith this drive does not reflect an innate propensity for power (although as we shall see, power also enters into the psychological foundation), but derives from our need to gain social esteem, to win the approbation of our fellow men. In a society that has, for historical reasons, chosen the path of capital accumulation, the approbation comes from the social value placed on wealth.[1]

But power enters as a motive too. It is disguised in the form of a natural propensity to acquiesce in social rank—that is, to accept the given class structure with its uneven distribution of wealth. In Smith's initial stage of "rude" society, he perceives, as do modern anthropologists, that there exists no substantial property in the means of production, and that there is therefore no basis for social differentiation in wealth. Matters change when society moves from its original rude state into a condition of nomadism that Smith imagines to be its first stratified form:

> It is in the age of shepherd, in the second period of society, that the inequality of fortune first begins to take place, and introduces among men a degree of authority and subordination which could not possibly exist before. It thereby introduces some degree of civil government which is indispensably necessary for its own preservation; and it seems to do this naturally, and even independent of the consideration of that necessity.[2]

"Civil government," he therefore concludes, "so far as it is instituted for the security of property, is in reality instituted for the defence of the rich against the poor, or

1. Smith, *Wealth,* p. 674.
2. Ibid., p. 674.

of those who have some property against those who have none at all."[3]

This is as unvarnished a description of a society of class domination as Marx could wish for. What is missing from this description are two things, which in fact separate the idea of a "society of natural liberty" from that of "capitalism." First, there is no awareness of the violent processes of social change required to produce the propertyless workforce on which is based the wage relation with its profit "share" that accrues to the capitalist.[4] Second, the attitude of subordination is taken as a fixed and necessary aspect of human nature. As a result, the *Wealth* can take for granted the stability—and, again, necessity—of the social domination implicit in the "sharing" of surplus, without any sense of exposing a relationship that is subject to radical challenge. Just as there are contests between masters and workmen featured in the *Wealth* without any conception of a "class struggle," so the clear admission of class inequalities as a precondition for accumulation involves no recognition of any political vulnerability of that process. Domination simply enters Smith's schema as a state of historic affairs, not as a social condition that requires constant reassertion and revindication through the successful pursuit of the accumulation process itself. That is why the accumulation of capital can be regarded by Smith as a means to an end—the end being the opulence

---

3. Ibid.

4. Ibid., p. 49.

of the larger society and the liberty of its members—and not as itself the end and purpose of society, to which both its opulence and its liberties are subordinate.

II

I have said enough to indicate how deep, far ranging, and even "Marxian" is Smith's vision of the psychological and social substratum on which accumulation rests. Equally prescient is Smith's view of the relation of government to the economy.

Smith lays out the relationship in a passage of great clarity. Having discussed and discarded the principles of mercantilism and physiocracy with their favored mercantile and agricultural elements, Smith concludes (with my italicized emphasis):

> All systems, either of preference or of restraint, therefore, being thus completely taken away, the obvious and simple system of natural liberty establishes itself of its own accord. Every man, as long as he does not violate the laws of justice, is left perfectly free to pursue his own interest in any way, and to bring both his industry and his capital into competition with those of any other man, or order of men. The sovereign is completely discharged from a duty, in the attempting to perform which he must always be exposed to innumerable delusions, and for the proper performance of which no human wisdom or knowledge could ever be sufficient; *the duty of superintending the industry of private people, and of directing it towards the employments most suitable to the interest of society.* According to the system of natural liberty, the sovereign has only three duties to attend to; three duties of great importance, indeed, but plain and intelligible to common understandings: first, the duty of protecting society from the violence and invasion of other independent

societies; secondly, the duty of protecting, as far as possible, every member of society from the injustice or oppression of every other member of it; and, thirdly, *the duty of erecting and maintaining certain public works and public institutions, which it can never be for the interest of any individual, or small number of individuals, to erect and maintain; because the profit could never repay the expence to any individual, nor small number of individuals, although it may frequently do much more than repay it to the greater society.*[5]

The passage is famous for establishing the minimal—indeed, minimalist—requirements of government within a society of perfect liberty. It is a description of government that deliberately seeks to reduce its importance, above all with respect to the activities that have now been relegated to the economic sphere. Thus, *The Wealth of Nations* is always, and quite correctly, regarded as a charter document in the schism of realms that is the most generally recognized politico-economic aspect of capitalism.

But this basic contention, which is clearly the immediate intent of Smith's argument, must be reexamined from the viewpoint of a concealed ambiguity of functions within each realm. Then it can be seen that the schism of realms is entirely consistent with the mixing of political and economic tasks characteristic of capitalism. Consider the admonition that government abandon the task of "superintending the industry of private people and of directing it toward the employments most suitable to the interest of society." The act of relinquishing the functions does not change their character. While they were performed by

5. Ibid., p. 651.

government, these acts provided the needed discipline of the labor force and the appropriate allocation of resources. Both these acts were evidently "political," insofar as they expressed the will of the sovereign. Now the functions are delegated to the private realm where they are performed under the aegis of market forces and the universalized quest for income. But the functions themselves—discipline and allocation—remain unchanged allthough the agencies that carry them out are now private rather than public. Thus Smith implicitly describes, although he certainly does not explicitly recognize, the transfer of "political" functions to the private realm that is peculiar to capitalism.

Even more significant is the second passage I have italicized. Here Smith prescribes, in words that have become classic, the rule that government should carry out only those economic activities necessary for the functioning of the larger society. What he fails to probe deeply are the implications of his own criteria for selecting those activities and projects that are suitable for undertaking by the state. The answer, as Smith's analysis itself makes clear, has nothing to do with the intrinsic nature of those "public" works or institutions. That is, there is no moral or political criterion that determines which activities are to be reserved for government and which not. The choice is solely based on the possibility of embracing each activity within the private accumulation circuit. Thus, were it profitable to sell the light that radiates from a lighthouse, beacons would become private enterprises; and were it not possible profitably to sell the output of the soil, farming would become perforce a public undertaking.

Smith's injunction to the state, therefore, is in fact an admonition to assume the "losses" that would accrue to whatever activities are deemed necessary, but unsuited for private organization. It is not a rule that limits the scope of public activity so much as one that defines it. The criteria are the technical possibilities of recapturing expenditures as private receipts—the possibility of *selling* output—and the judgment as to the importance of the activity itself for the viability of a society of natural liberty. Both vary, according to technology and organization, and to changing standards of social judgment. It is not surprising that Smith did not see this intermingling of public and private functions, engaged as he was in an effort to separate the two realms as widely as possible. What is remarkable is the ease with which we can infer from his own descriptions and prescriptions the bifurcation of roles that are in fact implied in the specification of a capitalist order.

III

Now what of the logic of the system?* It follows, as we shall see, from Smith's version of its nature—that is, from his understanding of its institutional and behavioral character.

The scenario begins in the central locus of the *Wealth*, the pin factory deprecatingly described by Smith as a "trifling manufacture." As many commentators have

*I have dealt here exclusively with the macrologic—the growth scenario—of the *Wealth,* not with its even more famous micrologic by which the allocation of goods and incomes is determined. The latter plays an indispensible role in keeping the growth process in balance, but it does not directly impel or govern that process. Hence its neglect in these pages.

pointed out, it was Smith's genius to have discerned the importance of manufacturing as a strategic center of the developmental process at a time when agriculture was still by far the most prevalent form of productive economic activity, and when manufacture itself accounted for no more than about ten percent of England's income. Here, within this famous ten-man establishment, we find the main source of the system's logic—its behavioral patterns, its technical enablements and constraints; the source of its self-regulative force of competition, its most threatening dysfunctions and its most promising attainments; and finally, the staging ground for the leap into the next period of capitalist maturation.

Smith tells us a great deal, although not everything, about the institutional setting of the pin factory. He traces the availability of its labor supply to the historic fact that most working people require a "master" to provide their subsistence. He makes explicit, as we have seen, the motivation of social esteem that will induce the master to seek to accumulate capital, and he is also explicit about the imbalance of class power that makes available to the capitalist his profit "share." Thus man and master come together in the pin factory under conditions that yield the master a profit which he will now use to "augment his fortune," rather than dissipating it in higher consumption.

To augment his fortune requires that the revenues of the establishment—the source of his profit share—be increased. This necessitates that sales increase, since no small manufacturer can raise his prices, lest customers buy from his competitors. To enlarge his sales, therefore, the capitalist uses part of his profit share to hire more workers, and part to equip them with the machines that play so critical a role in the next step of the process.

This next step involves the "division of labor"—the truncation of extended or complex tasks into shorter or simpler subtasks, each of which can be more rapidly ("dextrously") performed, without time being wasted in "sauntering" from one task to another, and each of which can be assisted by the complementary use of machines and equipment.

Smith does not mention another source of increased productivity—the ability to extract more labor energies from a work force gathered under the watchful eye of an overseer, and organized and disciplined in a quasi-military manner. Yet a main reason for the invention of the factory was the increase in production that ensued from this militarization of labor. "A hundred looms in families will not weave as much as ten, at least, consistently employed under the immediate supervision of a workman," wrote the first successful textile entrepreneur in New England in 1809.[6] The productivity gain of the division of labor must therefore be ascribed to an intensification of energies, in a manner that can be best likened to a forced march.

As the sum of all these causes, we realize the triumphant performance celebrated by Smith in the opening pages of the *Wealth,* where we see the pin factory at work. The famous passage is worth reproducing in extenso:

> . . . I have seen a small manufactory . . . where ten men only were employed, and where some of them consequently per-

---

6. Victor Clark, *History of Manufactures in the United States* (1929), p. 432.

formed two or three distinct operations. But though they were very poor, and therefore but indifferently accommodated with the necessary machinery, they could, when they exerted themselves, make among them about twelve pounds of pins in a day. There are in a pound upwards of four thousand pins of a middling size. Those ten persons, therefore, could make among them upwards of forty-eight thousand pins in a day. Each person, therefore, making a tenth part of forty-eight thousand pins, might be considered as making four thousand eight hundred pins in a day. But if they had all wrought separately and independently . . . , they certainly could not each of them have made twenty, perhaps not one pin in a day . . .[7]

The division of labor has complex side effects, as we shall see. But the unfolding of the logic hinges on the interplay between the *physical* consequence of the division of labor and its *economic* effect.[8] The physical consequence is the multiplication of output, generalized throughout the society. The economic effect is the chain of market repercussions that results from these altered technical flows. Initially this takes the form of a pressure for higher wages—the unintended outcome of a general demand for labor needed for accumulation. But this threat to profits is now offset by a second link in the chain. Smith foresees that the wage increase will be held within acceptable bounds because the higher wages of the working force will enlarge the supply of child labor, child labor being recognized as a regular source of labor power. The effect of the increased demand for labor is therefore to augment

7. Smith, *Wealth,* pp. 4, 5.

8. This explication of Smith's logic was first presented by Adolph Lowe in "The Classical Theory of Economic Growth," *Social Research,* vol. 21, 1954, pp. 127–158, and again in his *On Economic Knowledge,* ch. 6.

the supply of labor, "[the] liberal reward for labor [enabling the poor] to provide better for their children, and consequently to bring up a greater number . . ." In turn the greater number force the price of labor "to that proper rate which the circumstances of societies require. It is in this manner that the demand for men, like that for any other commodity, necessarily regulates the production of men."[9]

This now completes one chain of economic consequences: the larger demand for labor bringing forth a matching supply, which assures that the accumulation process will not be blocked by a prohibitively steep wage increase. The economic logic now reinforces the logic of technology. The stabilizing influence on wage rates makes possible a continuation of the process of hiring, and this in turn creates a growing volume of workers' spending power, a constituent part of the "market" to which the employer caters. As the market grows, it becomes possible for the employer to divide and mechanize his labor process still further, since the degree of technical advance, in Smith's well-known phrase, "is limited by the extent of the market." Thus, the successful overcoming of a threatened squeeze on profits establishes the conditions for a continuation of the technical advance on which the momentum of the system is ultimately based. The process is self-sustaining, self-feeding, seamless—in Schumpeter's words apparently "hitchless."[10]

Actually Smith does not project a hitchless scenario for

---

9. Smith, *Wealth,* pp. 79, 80.

10. Joseph Schumpeter, *History of Economic Analysis* (1952), pp. 572, 640.

the long term. The very technology of the pin factory suggests a limitation that must attend an accumulation process dependent on the multiplication of pin factories. There will sooner or later be no more need for pins; profits will fall; accumulation will halt. "As capitals increase in any country," Smith writes,

> the profits which can be made by employing them necessarily diminish. It becomes gradually more and more difficult to find within the country a profitable means of employing new capital. There arises in consequence a competition between different capitals, the owner of one endeavouring to get possession of that employment which is occupied by another.[11]

Finally, therefore, accumulation ceases because "as great a quantity of stock [is] employed in every branch as the nature and extent of the trade would admit. The competition, therefore, would every-where be very great, and consequently the ordinary profit as low as possible."[12] The laboring class, meanwhile, continues the high rate of reproduction brought about by above-minimal subsistance, bringing additional numbers of workers into the market and thereby depressing the wage rate. A harsh prospect thus impends: "In a country which has acquired that full complement of riches which the nature of its soil and climate, and its situation with respect to other countries, allowed it to acquire; which could therefore advance no further, and which was not going backward, both the

---

11. Smith, *Wealth,* p. 336.
12. Ibid., p. 95.

wages of labor and the profits of stock would probably be very low."[13]

"Perhaps no country has ever yet arrived at this degree of opulence," Smith continues.[14] Nonetheless, the explicit threat has been squarely posed, although implicitly relegated to the distant future. The threat is that of a saturation of demand and an end to accumulation. In one form or another, that threat haunted all the observers of early capitalism, who successively brought the day of saturation closer. Ricardo believed that stagnation would rapidly overtake the growth process unless cheap food imports permitted wages to be reduced; John Stuart Mill, writing in the mid-nineteenth century, saw profits only a "hand's breadth" above the threshold of necessary profitability. Thus the logic of accumulation of early capitalism was emphatically not one of indefinite growth, but rather of growth limited by finite, exhaustible investment possibilities. In Smith's case the outlook was worsened because the continued increase of population, after accumulation halted, implied a deterioration of workers' real living standards, not merely the attainment of a static equilibrium.

IV

We will defer until the end of this chapter a further consideration of this vision. For there are problems with regard to the internal consistency and cogency of Smith's logic that must be considered if we are to assess his schema

13. Ibid., p. 94.
14. Ibid., p. 95.

as a guide to historical reality. Here it is useful to begin with technology, at first glance the most "mechanical" and self-evident element in Smith's logical chain. What is critical here is the nature of the technological process that Smith envisages. This takes the form of equipping an *increased* work force, whose larger number enables the work process to be more finely subdivided, with machinery that will support or quicken their tasks. "The number of workmen in every branch of industry generally increases with the division of labour in that branch," writes Smith, "or rather, it is the increase of their number which enables them to class and subdivide themselves in this manner."[15]

What is crucial in this depiction is that the labor-attracting division of labor extends the market through the larger payrolls that it generates, thereby providing the necessary economic basis for further technical and organizational progress. As Lowe has pointed out, if the technical aspects of mechanization were differently conceived, this would not be the case. Then the machinery would not stand beside the increasingly dextrous, stationary worker to augment his or her abilities, but would displace the worker entirely. The flow of product would not diminish, but the flow of waged purchasing power would. The hitchless matching of economic demand and physical supply would be replaced by an uneven contest between rising supply, and stagnant or even contracting workers' demand. The scenario would shift in decisive ways from one of steady growth to one of actual or incipient crisis occasioned by the failure of workers' income to support the rise

15. Ibid., p. 260.

of mass production. In a word, the logic of the *Wealth of Nations* would be replaced by that of *Capital.*

The specific characteristics of Smith's technology play yet a further role in assuring a smooth trajectory because of the manner in which they affect competition. The pin factory illustration suggests a huge effect on output from the division and mechanization of labor, but the fact of the matter is that the multiplicative effect of Smith's mechanization is limited. The limitations reside in two aspects of the mechanization process. First, mechanization does not lower the costs of "pioneering" manufacturers so rapidly as to allow the first in line to gather the whole market for himself. This seems surprising, in that Smith's pin factory, by his own figures, increases the productivity of a laborer by a factor between two hundred and forty and four thousand eight hundred—surely enough to establish the first pin maker as a monopolist in his field. But the process of capital accumulation that we have traced makes it evident that this is not envisaged as a sudden leap, but a gradual ascent. Pin making improves man by man and machine by machine, so despite the immense jump from artisanal production, the rate of technological change, and its associated competitive advantage, is restrained.

A second implicit limitation of Smith's technology is that it does not seek consciously to modify the product radically, but rather to improve and cheapen it. The mechanized pin factory continues to turn out pins, and does not threaten to restructure the nature and extent of the market by introducing some wholly different end product, such as clips or snaps or safety pins. That potentially destabilizing effect of technology, in which a new product wipes out a whole branch of industry, will be deferred to the period of middle capitalism, along with discontinuous leaps in technology that enable pioneers radically to lower costs through the redesign of their production flows. Together with the rise of labor-displacing machinery, it will be just such new technological capabilities that decisively separate middle from early capitalism.

Yet another mitigating aspect of the competitive struggle in early capitalism was that much of the impact of the new technology fell on the precapitalist sector rather than on the manufacturers themselves. In the early nineteenth century a considerable volume of production was still carried on by cottage industry in various forms, so that the growing volume of output exerted much of its leveling force against the frail establishments of artisanates, homemade yarns and cloths, and small-scale family undertakings, all of which were easy casualties to the expansive power of incipient machinofacture.

These unnoticed constraints of the technology of early capitalism have important consequences for the working out of the Smithian logic. Specifically, they lessen and mitigate the mutual encroachment of capitals that is the inevitable result of their generalized expansion, so that competition assumes the benign guise of a disciplinary process—the "only source of good management" says Smith,[16]—rather than a malign and disturbing element. To put it differently, the cutthroat competition that will be a major element in *Capital* does not appear in the *Wealth.* We see empirical evidence of this when we note the slow

16. Ibid., p. 147.

pace at which individual capitals expanded during the period of early capitalism. As late as 1851 two-thirds of the English textile mills still employed less than 50 workers, and the average mill less than 200,[17] and the United States census of 1869 showed the average number of employees in a manufacturing establishment in that year to be still below ten.[18] This could not have been the case was not the technology of the period only a moderate force for individual plant expansion.

V

With all its unavoidable shortcomings, Smith's overall scenario is a stunning exercise in social analysis, insofar as it does indeed attempt to ground its model-like logic in the substratum of explicitly described motivations and institutions. The success is all the clearer because Smith's logic has only one major prediction that applies to the economic realm, narrowly construed. This is the logic of technical and economic interactions that results in long-term, sustained growth, "hitchless" or not. It hardly warrants saying that this prediction has been amply confirmed by the trend of events. In all early capitalisms the rate of growth of output rises, often dramatically, as these nations "take off," in W.W. Rostow's phrase, under the impetus of the reciprocating engines of technical improvement and economic stimulus. In the case of Great Britain total output leaped from a ten-year average rate of only 2.7 percent in the 1770s (it had been more than double that in the previ-

17. David Landes, *The Unbound Prometheus* (1969), p. 121.

18. *Historical Statistics of the United States* (1975), Series P1, P4, P5.

ous decade) to well over 20 percent in the decades of the 1780s and 1790s, and jumps of roughly similar magnitude followed a few decades later as the industrial techniques of England found their way to the Continent, despite considerable efforts on the part of England to prevent their export.[19]

A second aspect of the Smith scenario that can be tested against history is the interplay between the demand for and supply of labor—the supply rising fast enough to prevent a serious check to accumulation from higher wages. Here the basic facts are congruent with the scenario. Population rose markedly throughout the period of early capitalism. In England and Wales the rate of increase in the 1820s was almost five times that of the 1740s; on the Continent the rise in population in the early nineteenth century was dramatic, France growing from 27.5 millions in 1801 to 34 millions in 1850; Germany from 23.5 millions in 1810 to 33.5 millions at mid-century.[20]

The causes of this population rise were manifold. It was not due to rising wages, as Smith's logic implied, but it seems indisputable that it could not have taken place without the increase in the quantity of food and other necessary outputs that early capitalism brought. What is important is that the mutually supportive interaction of labor supply and labor-requiring technical progress allowed the growth process to unfold in the manner described by

---

19. W. W. Rostow, *The World Economy* (1980), p. 378, Table V-3, p. 388, Table V-6, pp. 391, 392, 395, Table V-8, pp. 397, 401, 601.

20. Phillis Deane, *The First Industrial Revolution* (1965), p. 32; Landes, *Unbound Prometheus,* p. 152.

Smith. Phyllis Deane, looking back over the period, writes:

> It seems reasonable to suppose that without the growth of output dating from the 1740s the associated growth in population would eventually have been checked by a rise in the death rate due to declining standards of living. It seems equally probable that without the population growth which gathered momentum in the second half of the eighteenth century, the British industrial revolution would have been retarded for lack of labour. It seems likely that without the rising demand and prices which reflected, *inter alia,* the growth of population, there would have been less incentive for British producers to expand and innovate, and hence some of the dynamism which powered the industrial revolution would have been lost. It seems equally likely that the expanding employment opportunities created by the industrial revolution encouraged people to marry and produce families earlier than in the past, and that they increased the average expectation of life.[21]

If we substitute "early capitalism" for "the industrial revolution," Deane's reconstruction of historical events dovetails very well with the master scenario. That the increase in population served to hold back wage increases seems beyond dispute. The scanty data we possess rule out precise estimates of working class standards, but there is a consensus against any perceptible improvement prior to 1820, the very period in which hundreds of thousands of men, women, and children entered factory employment. Indeed, it is probable that the opposite was the case: "On balance," Deane concludes, "average standards of living tended to fall rather than to rise." This was in part the

---

21. Deane, *First Industrial Revolution,* p. 34.

consequence of poor harvests and war shortages, but it was also due to floods of workers that held back wage increases. In 1792 the cotton weavers of Manchester were making 15s. to 20s. per week, but these boom wages attracted so many more laborers (as Smith says, "the demand for men, like that for any other commodity, necessarily regulates the production of men") that by 1800 a workman toiling 14 hours a day could earn only 5s. to 6s. per week.[22] The stabilization of workers' living standards would not come until the end of the period, and would thereby constitute another of the forces that ushered in the different scenario of middle capitalism.

VI

The matter of workers' living standards brings us to an aspect of Smith's conspectus that we have until now allowed to pass unnoticed. This was the effect of the technology of the pin factory, not on physical output, or economic demand, but on the moral and psychological condition of the worker exposed to its demands and rhythms. Smith is characteristically outspoken about the matter. The quotation on page 97, above, reads in full:

> In the progress of the division of labour, the employment of the far greater part of those who live by labour, that is, of the great body of the people, comes to be confined to a few very simple operations, frequently to one or two. But the understand-

22. Ibid., p. 250, and citations on pp. 248 and 251; regarding Manchester weavers, p. 244. See also E. P. Thompson, *The Making of the English Working Class* (1952), p. 318.

ings of the greater part of men are necessarily formed by their ordinary employments. The man whose whole life is spent in performing a few simple operations, of which the effects too are, perhaps, always the same, or very nearly the same, has no occasion to exert his understanding, or to exercise his invention in finding out expedients for removing difficulties which never occur. He naturally loses, therefore, the habit of such exertion, and generally becomes as stupid and ignorant as it is possible for a human creature to become. The torpor of his mind renders him, not only incapable of relishing or bearing a part in any rational conversation, but of conceiving any generous, noble, or tender sentiment, and consequently of forming any just judgment concerning many even of the ordinary duties of private life. Of the great and extensive interests of his country he is altogether incapable of judging; and unless very particular pains have been taken to render him otherwise, he is equally incapable of defending his country in war. . . . His dexterity at his own particular trade seems, in this manner, to be acquired at the expence of his intellectual, social, and martial virtues. . . .[23]

Thus the division of labor, the form of work organization that holds the main promise of improvement for a society of liberty, becomes the source of its most seriously debilitating dysfunction. Smith is plain about this: "These are the disadvantages of a commercial spirit," he had lectured in 1762. "The minds of men are contracted and rendered incapable of elevation, education is despised or at most neglected, and the heroic spirit is almost utterly extinguished." In the *Wealth* he writes that this stultification threatens "the almost entire corruption and degeneracy of the great body of the people," and the rise of a

---

23. Smith, *Wealth,* pp. 734, 735.

working population in which "all the nobler parts of the human character may be, in a great measure, obliterated and extinguished."[24]

Smith therefore locates the central problem of early capitalism in the undermining of a successful, although not limitless, logic of capital accumulation by the deterioration of social life produced by that very accumulative process. *The basic contradiction of the society of natural liberty was therefore social and moral, not economic.*

Smith attributes these deformations to industrial processes—comparing, for example, the dull condition of the industrial worker with the alert intelligence of members of "barbarous" societies.[25] He did not clearly see that the division of labor was an organizational form dictated by the need of capital accumulation. His contemporary, Adam Ferguson, looked more deeply in this matter. "Manufactures prosper most," he wrote in his *Essay on Civil Society,* "where the mind is least consulted, and where the workshop may, without any great effort of the imagination, be considered as an engine, the parts of which are men."[26] What Ferguson glimpsed was that the technology of the pin factory was shaped for the purpose of prosperous manufacture—that the truncation of labor, with its dehumanizing amplication by machine power and its mindless repetitiveness, was not the consequence of an

---

24. 1762 citation from Adam Smith, *Lectures on Jurisprudence* (1978), p. 541. *Wealth,* p. 736.

25. Smith, *Wealth,* p. 735.

26. Adam Ferguson, *An Essay on Civil Society* (1966), p. 183.

absolute imperative of technology itself, but of a technology pressed into the service of capital accumulation.

VII

Were Smith's expectations in regard to the degradation of the working class as unambiguously borne out by history as his expectations with regard to the mutually supportive action of technology and economics? Here the answer is surprising. Anyone familiar with the disastrous decline in working class conditions during early capitalism, both within factory life and in the new factory towns, will be impressed with the prescience of Smith's vision. At second look, however, the degradation of the working class was not that which Smith expected. The brutality, not merely the monotony of work; the decline in real wages that lasted until in the 1820s; the rise of the industrial slum that drew from de Tocqueville the remark that "civilization works its miracles and civilized man is turned back almost into a savage"[27]—all these were failures of a kind that Smith failed completely to foresee. These *material*—not moral—consequences of rapid accumulation were not an integral part of Smith's scenario but were unquestionably an integral part of English (and and to a lesser extent of Continental) and American early capitalist history.

More surprising, the very drudgery that Smith expected to quench the "martial spirit" of the working class produced instead that least imagined result—the rise of a

27. Cited in E. Hobsbawm, *Industry and Empire* (1968), pp. 67–68.

working class consciousness capable of formulating interests distinct from, although not quite frontally opposed to, those of the dominant bourgeois class. Smith had spoken of the condition of the laborer as making him "incapable of either comprehending [society's] interest, or of understanding its connexion with his own."[28] Yet that is precisely what the dynamics of the accumulation process brought. In *The Making of the English Working Class,* E. P. Thompson has told the story of the gradual coalescing of fragmented understandings and indignations into a political movement seeking to "exert the power of the [working] class to humanize the environment . . . not for profit, but for *use.*"[29] On the Continent, the ill-fated uprisings of 1848—launched in a fervor of naive socialist enthusiasm that proved a turning point in the intellectual development of Marx and Engels—nevertheless gave evidence that the workingman was not stupefied by the conditions of his labor, so much as awakened and incensed by them.

None of these movements culminated in a serious threat to the legitimacy of the social order, although in England and the Continent they raised momentary fears of social revolution. Their presence throughout early capitalism testifies, however, to the failure of Smith's logic to embrace the full significance of the contradiction that he correctly located in the tension between the material and the moral conditions of production. Viewing the social order, as Smith did, from the conceptual basis of a society

28. Smith, *Wealth,* p. 249.

29. Thompson, *Making of the English Working Class,* p. 830 (italics in text).

of natural liberty in which the domination of the existing class was never put into question, it is understandable that he should have seen the repercussions of the capitalist organization of production as giving rise only to a deterioration, not to an awakening or strengthening, of the resolve—the "martial spirit"—of the laborer. Here is, of course, a manifest consequence of his bounded vision. Had he perceived more fully the nature of capital itself, above all the historical processes by which its social powers were created, he might have viewed differently the history-shaping potential of labor, the creature of capital; but such an insight would have been at total variance with the world view of the Enlightenment in which societies and civilizations rose and fell, but the subordination of the lower classes remained.

VII

Thus the *Wealth of Nations* unfolds its stylized history in two intertwined strands—a self-propelling, self-guiding expansion of output ending only when society has laid in its "full complement" of capital, and a long deterioration of moral well-being, generated by the very technology required to achieve material growth. There are, of course, other strands in Smith's logic, some of them of major importance, such as the allocation of resources to fit society's buying patterns, or the lodgement of England in the larger world economy. But it is time to make a summary judgment of the whole, to assess the adequacy of Smith's central chain of logic as an explanation of the historic trajectory of capitalism in its first industrial period.

At one level such a judgment is easy to make. With all

its errors of omission and commission, the *Wealth of Nations* is a remarkable effort to explain the development of a society in which the commanding presence of government had yielded, to an unprecedented degree, to the spontaneous interactions of many capitals. From this point of view what is astonishing about the *Wealth* is not its failure to appreciate the complexity of many social and technical processes, or to foresee the rise of a working class consciousness. The achievement is the degree to which Smith's conception of the nature of the system gives us a logic that can explain so much.

Curiously, it is the very cogency and power of analysis that leads to the final question we can put to Smith: how is it that the scenario he predicted did not run its bitter course, culminating in an end to accumulation, with all the horrendous consequences that would have accompanied such an historic failure? In the terms of our argument, only one explanation can be offered for the failure of history to reproduce Smith's logic. The nature of the system must have altered in ways that changed the logic itself. Thus, just as Smith's failure to anticipate the possibility of a growth of working class consciousness alerts us to deficiencies in the fundamental concept of a society of natural liberty, so the failure of society to reach a condition of saturation causes us to search out a corresponding inadequacy in some other equally central part of Smith's overall perception.

It is not difficult to see where this deficiency lies. It lodges in the failure to realize that the pin factory, the representative unit of capital that determines so much of the period's dynamics, is itself only a form of capital, and as such, subject to gradual, eventually irresistible pressures for change, precisely because the existing form threatens an end to accumulation. In a word, the pin factory gives way to the steel mill. An immense change in scale marks the difference between the two periods, a change associated with a new form of the labor process, new strategies and intensities of competition, new possibilities for commodification, and finally, new ideological and political functions and characteristics.

Was this transition itself presaged by the logic of the *Wealth?* Were the forces that created the steel mill already apparent, although unnoticed, in the pin factory? Such questions are the historians' bane, the setting for traps of many sorts, not least that of *post hoc, ergo propter hoc* reasoning, the tempting assumption to treat events as the only possible devolution of their antecedents, rather than as one among many possibilities, distinguished from its alternatives only because in fact it occurred.

It is this pitfall that suggests a way of dealing with the problem. It is to recognize that the original Smithian logic was entirely plausible, and the end to which it pointed entirely imaginable, *provided that the level of technology remained at the stage of development we find portrayed in the* Wealth of Nations. The technology of the pin factory—by which we mean in historic actuality, that of the cotton mill, the stationary steam engine, the puddling process for making wrought iron—offered very important but strictly limited possibilities for capital accumulation. The opportunities were important in creating vortices for the attraction of capital, but they were limited because, as we have seen, these vortices catered to essentially regional markets, with relatively modest increases in output, through the medium of largely unchanged final products.

To appreciate the limitations of the technology of early capitalism we must compare iron puddling with its small batches of output with the Bessemer converter and its vast cauldron of molten metal; the stream of output of pins with the Niagara of the cigarette machines; the capital requirement to make candles with that needed to supply household gas and then electric light; the possibilities inherent in stationary steam engines with those of moveable, even self-moving motors. These comparisons do not merely evoke different industrial or existential landscapes, but entirely different vistas for the accumulation of capital, for the mutual interaction of capitals, and for the alteration of the social environment.

The question then becomes whether there is a logic of technological progress, enabling us to anticipate, even if only in the most general way, the rate or direction of its change. From a micro point of view, there is little doubt that the answer is no. Confidently anticipated advances may stubbornly refuse to emerge; others occur where least expected. Cotton finds its gin; sugar cane resists all efforts to mechanize its harvest. Petroleum yields to science; coal does not. The railroad becomes the most economically significant form of transportation; the paved road lags far behind. Entertainment is an early candidate for commodification; education less so; health—save for quack remedies—hardly enters the accumulation circuit. Communication becomes possible at long distances, but technology brings no advances to mutual comprehension. Men discover means of conquering the oceans in cheap, seaworthy ships before they discover the means of erecting inexpensive houses. Fertilizers are developed quickly; pesticides much later. Thus technological progress, especially in the period of early capitalism, remains a highly personal adventure, its victories and defeats as unforeseeable as those of campaigns and battles in war.

Yet the very metaphor suggests that we must distinguish between the triumphs of individual technological inventions and innovations—even those that opened immense channels for capital accumulation—and the general tide of technological effort itself. It is the latter that is decisive. Under the regime of capital, even in its early period when technology assumes the simple forms of mechanization, the effort to discover opportunities for accumulation through alterations in the mode of manufacture becomes the objective of a thousand economic generals, not to mention ten thousand soldiers with field marshals' batons in their knapsacks—the Arkwrights and Watts and Wilkinsons of all nations. A generalized receptivity to technical change readies the economic actors for experimentation, rather than setting them against it as in the period of guild restrictions and anti-innovative artisan outlooks. Thus, while it is pointless or foolish to suggest that the Bessemer converter, the Bonsack cigarette machine, the Edison lamp, or the Otto gasoline engine had to appear when they did, or that close substitutes would have taken their place had they not, we can confidently assert that inventing itself is systematically stimulated by capitalism. From this point of view, the period of early capitalism should be seen as a staging era during which pressures accumulated for further technological changes

—eventually of sufficient importance to alter the technical and organizational fabric of the system and its logical path.

The essential omission from Smith's understanding then—and from that of Ricardo and John Stuart Mill—was the failure to perceive the intensity and ubiquity of the search for technological change as an intrinsic part of the regime of capital, a search that could not guarantee the success of its efforts, but that would infuse the system with a momentum unlikely to end because it had exhausted the possibilities of any given technical structure. It was Marx who saw the power of this inherent source of socioeconomic change, and who perceived the implications for the changeful logic of a system founded on so protean an element of its nature.

Smith's failure to grasp the immanent thrust of technology thus reflects a certain boundedness of his vision. This is different from the socio-political limitation that placed beyond the reach of his imagination any possibility of class *bouleversement.* It is a failure to perceive that the *economic* basis which he himself made central to his explication of emergent capitalism could not be adequately described merely as the desire to "better our condition." What is missing was a recognition that the accumulation of capital was for capitalists the imperious task of the legitimation of a regime. To point to this shortfall of his perceptions is not to lessen our admiration for Smith, whose penetration of the veil of economics puts to shame virtually all economic observers, but only to remind us that our analytic capability is based first and foremost on what we see.

7

Schumpeter's Vision

NO ECONOMIST was more aware of the presence and importance of Vision than Joseph Schumpeter, so let us explore the problem further, and also bait the trap, by reading what he has to say about the matter. "In every scientific venture," he wrote:

> the thing that comes first is Vision. That is to say, before embarking upon analytic work of any kind we must first single out the set of phenomena we wish to investigate, and acquire "intuitively" a preliminary notion of how they hang together or, in other words, of what appear from our standpoint to be fundamental properties. This should be obvious. If it is not, this is only owing to the fact that in practice we mostly do not start from a vision of our own but from the work of our predecessors or from ideas that float in the public mind.[1]

Without vision, then, the analytic work of economics could not begin. But what kind of vision? Is all analysis doomed to reflect the biases and prejudices of the observer? Schumpeter is acutely aware of that possibility, for he boldly moves from the high ground of vision—the

1. Schumpeter, *History of Economic Analysis,* p. 561–562.

unavoidable "preanalytic cognitive act"—to the low ground of ideology:

> Analytic work begins with material provided by our vision of things, and this vision is ideological almost by definition. It embodies the picture of things as we wish to see them, and wherever there is any possible motive for wishing to see them in a given rather than another light, the way we see things can hardly be distinguished from the way in which we wish to see them. The more honest and naive our vision is, the more dangerous is it to the eventual emergence of anything for which general validity can be claimed. The inference for the social sciences is obvious, and it is not even true that he who hates a social system will form an objectively more correct vision of it than he who loves it.[2]

What then protects vision from becoming "mere" ideology? The answer is the antiseptic effect of scientific work. "[T]he rules of procedure that we apply in our analytic work," Schumpeter continues, "are almost as much exempt from ideological influence as vision is subject to it. . . . [These rules] tend to crush out ideologically conditioned error from the visions with which we start."[3]

Thus the stage is set, and never more openly, in full view of the audience. Ideology-ridden vision peoples the theater with the dramatis personae of its own choosing, but the economist-author must nonetheless compose the drama according to the logic of the situation. Vision creates as it wishes, but scientific analysis proceeds as it must. Preanalytic cognition is thus accorded its essential role, but the

2. Ibid., p. 42–43.

3. Ibid., p. 43.

rules of scientific investigation preclude its use for whatever purposes we wish.

I

As with everything that Schumpeter writes, it is a bravura performance, and on the face of it a plausible one. Where better to test its usefulness, accordingly, than against the body of Schumpeter's own work? This will lead us into a brief recapitulation of key themes which I shall elaborate only to the point of making them comprehensible to someone not already familiar with them. For it is not the specific content of these themes that interests us so much as the contradictions and paradoxes openly contained in them—puzzles to which we shall have to look to vision and ideology for resolution.

This takes us initially to his *Theory of Economic Development,* first published in Germany in 1911—an analysis of capitalist dynamics whose most striking characteristic is its clash of two opposing, and indeed incompatible depictions of the capitalist process. The first of these is that of a socioeconomic system whose immanent tendency is to reach and maintain a condition of static equilibrium. Schumpeter describes this "circular flow" as a condition in which all agents have found positions that maximize for each the utilities or earnings made available by nature and knowledge. Thus the circular flow resembles the stationary state toward which Ricardo and Mill both saw the economy moving, although the latter two perceived it as a final destination for capitalism, whereas Schumpeter sees it as the position from which its historic trajectory begins.

Whether as terminus *ad quem* or *a quo,* the crucial economic aspect of the stationary economy is that the pressure of competition, coupled with the mobility of factors, removes any possibility of profit. In the visionary capitalism of perfect competition, workers will be paid the full value of their product; and owners of resources will claim the rents that correspond to the "opportunity costs" of their resources in other employments. But the owners of capital, whether money or equipment, will not earn a rental return, although they may, if they are also active managers, receive the wages of management. They will receive nothing beyond these wages because the capital equipment they buy is a manmade product (unlike natural resources), and the price that capitalists must pay for it under ideal competition will therefore completely absorb the value of its contribution to output, exactly like the wages of labor. It also follows that the absence of any such profit margin removes any incentive for a borrower to pay a fee (interest) for command over funds.[4] As part of this profitless circular flow, we should also note that the system is characterized above all else by its inertial tendency. Minor adjustments will take place as agents react to adventitious changes in the economic environment—vagaries of the weather, as it were—but no structural changes disturb the peaceful reproductive process, above all, not that of technological change.

Thus our first explicit and conscious Schumpeterian vision is that of capitalism as a changeless, profitless socio-

4. Joseph Schumpeter, *The Theory of Economic Development* (1946), pp. 30–31.

economic system. Note that this vision hinges on the motives that keep the system "revolving." These motives bear little resemblance to the active maximizing we find in contemporary economic theorizing. In Schumpeter's circular flow, routine and custom provide the motive force for business behavior, rather than a never-ending search for advantage. The point is important enough to warrant citing the relevant passages at some length:

> When [the individual] makes decisions concerning his economic conduct he does not pay attention to all the facts . . . in this value [price] system. . . . He acts in the ordinary daily round according to general custom and experience, and in every use of a given good, he starts from its value which is given to him by experience. . . . The value system once established and the combinations once given are always the starting point for every new economic period and have so to speak a presumption in their favor.
>
> This stability is indispensable for the economic conduct of individuals. In practice they could not, in by far the majority of the cases, do the mental labor necessary to create this experience anew.[5]

Thus inertia is the great guide for action, the "geology" of experience, in economic life as elsewhere. As Schumpeter puts it:

> [A]ll knowledge and habit once acquired become as firmly rooted in ourselves as a railway embankment in the earth. It does not require to be continually renewed and consciously reproduced, but sinks into the strata of subconsciousness. . . . Everything we think, feel, or do often enough becomes automatic and our conscious life is unburdened of it. . . . This holds

5. Ibid., pp. 39, 40.

good likewise for economic daily life. And from this it follows also for economic life that every step outside the boundary of routine has difficulties and involves a new element. It is this element that constitutes the phenomenon of leadership.[6]

The last word sounds the countertheme that will now compose the great fugue of capitalist development. This is the famous depiction of capitalism as a system whose characteristic and distinctive attribute is not inertia but change, not routine but a "perennial gale of creative destruction."[7]

How can we account for this second vision, so utterly at odds with the first? Here we encounter the key *dramatis persona* of Schumpeter's counter-vision. It is the entrepreneur, the economic agent who will dynamize the system. Only the entrepreneur has the will, the intelligence, and the force of character to break the mold of custom and tradition. He vitalizes the circular flow either by introducing new products or processes into it, or by recombining factors in ways that enable him to produce existing outputs more cheaply than the competition.

Unfortunately, the act of economic leadership does not earn for the entrepreneur the "affective values which are the glory of all other kinds of social leadership," such as military or political. The entrepreneur fulfills a task "which only in very rare cases appeals to the imagination of the public." Indeed, he "moves about in society as an upstart, whose ways are readily laughed at."[8]

---

6. Ibid, p. 84. For inertia as a specific property of "the psyche of the businessman," see page 86. We will return to this below.

7. Joseph Schumpeter, *Capitalism, Socialism, and Democracy* (1942), p. 84.

8. Schumpeter, *Theory of Economic Development*, pp. 89, 90.

Why, then, do some individuals undertake the thankless tasks of entrepreneurship? Schumpeter answers:

> First of all there is the dream and the will to found a private kingdom, usually, although not necessarily, also a dynasty. The modern world really does not know any such positions, but what may be attained by industrial or commercial success is still the nearest approach to medieval lordship possible to modern man. Its fascination is especially strong for people who have no other chance of achieving social distinction. . . .
>
> Then there is the will to conquer: the impulse to fight, to prove oneself superior to others, to succeed for the sake, not of the fruits of success, but of success itself. . . . And again we are faced with a motivation characteristically different from that of "satisfaction of wants." . . .
>
> Finally, there is the joy of creating, of getting things done, or simply of exercising one's energy and ingenuity. This is akin to a ubiquitous motive, but nowhere does it stand out as an independent factor of behavior with anything like the clearness with which it obtrudes itself in our case. Our type seeks out difficulties, changes in order to change, delights in ventures. . . .
>
> Only with the first groups of motives is private property as the result of entrepreneurial activity an essential factor in making it operative. With the other two it is not. . . .[9]

We now have the constituent parts of Schumpeter's two visions of capitalism. On the one hand capitalism is portrayed as an essentially inert form of economic society, a circular flow, where the function of the capitalist is entirely that of managing, in a routine fashion, the resources that have come under his control. In fact it is unclear what role a capitalist *qua* capitalist could play in such a bizarre

---

9. Ibid., p. 93, 94.

"capitalism," since Schumpeter asserts that his money would earn no interest and his productive equipment no profit. Rents of resources would absorb the entire surplus of aggregate sales price over aggregate payrolls. The euthanasia of the rentier, of which Keynes spoke in the *General Theory,* would be replaced under the regime of a circular flow capitalism by the euthanasia of the capitalist.

But this is only the first vision. The second concerns the destruction of the inertial properties of capitalism under the impetus of its entrepreneurs. Their creation of profitable enterprises not only moves the system off dead center, but establishes the need for credit, by which new capital formation takes place. The highly uneven distribution and the scarcity of talent lead to the phenomenon of "swarming," as less innovative entrepreneurs follow on the heels of the pioneering leaders. From this follows a theory of the business cycle, set forth in two volumes in *Business Cycles* (1939).

The cogency of this economic analysis does not interest us here.[10] Rather, we review the well-known scenario only to stress that its underlying theoretical structure—the tension between the circular flow and the expansionism of the dynamized system—rests on ideal types that Schumpeter has perceived in or projected into the social mists. Without the conception of the routinizing economic agent, including the "normal" business person, there would be no circular flow. Without the conception of an innovating

10. *Business Cycles* attempts to survey economic history in support of a theory of "swarming" as a fundamental explanation of the business cycle. The claim is widely rejected.

and pioneering entrepreneur there would be no gale of creative destruction. Schumpeter's theory thus appears to derive, as he himself warned us to expect, from preanalytic cognitive acts out of which the elements of the theory are formed. That these acts are also ideological seems equally uncontestable. The entrepreneur is manifestly a personality type with whom Schumpeter feels a close affinity. The heroic role into which he is cast therefore gives to capitalism a swashbuckling, adventuresome flavor that is also much in keeping with Schumpeter's own flamboyant personality. The ideological aspect of the vision is therefore no more than an instantiation of Schumpeter's often-expressed admiration of bourgeois civilization. Vision and ideology make coherent the clash of static and dynamic. The way has been cleared for the exercise of pure analysis.

II

Is that in fact the resolution of the matter? I think not. Schumpeter was, after all, perfectly aware of the contradictoriness of his two "visions" of capitalism as circular flow and as creative destruction, and he wrote extensively about the tragicomic figure of the entrepreneur. To ground his analysis on such manifestly conscious perceptions and preferences reduces the idea of vision and ideology to trivial—or at any rate, not very interesting—proportions. The very clarity of Schumpeter's clashing economic tendencies and the unequivocal favor accorded to the pioneering entrepreneur suggest that there is a deeper level of preanalytic cognition at work—a level to which Schumpeter's conscious attention does not descend, or of which he may indeed have been entirely unaware.

Such a level exists, I believe, if we scrutinize Schumpeter's work for a Vision—I capitalize the word to stress its distance from the conscious visions we have already discussed—that underlies the circular flow, the idea of creative destruction, and the entrepreneur, a Vision that precedes, as it were, the conscious depictions of ideal-types from which his explicit analysis proceeds. Such a deep Vision exists, as I shall attempt to show, in Schumpeter's view of "history" as the product of social elites.

A theory of elites presupposes a theory of the distribution of human talents and capabilities. Let us therefore examine Schumpeter's statements about the matter.

> Now these aptitudes are presumably distributed in an ethnically homogeneous population just like others, that is the curve of their distribution has a maximum ordinate, deviations on either side of which become rarer the greater they are. Similarly we can assume that every healthy man can sing if he will. Perhaps half the individuals in an ethnically homogeneous group have the capacity for it to an average degree, a quarter in progressively diminishing measure, and, let us say, a quarter in a measure above average; and within this quarter, through a series of continually increasing singing ability and continually diminishing number of people who possess it, we come finally to the Carusos. . . .
>
> Let us apply this: Again, a quarter of the population may be so poor in those qualities, let us say here provisionally of economic initiative that the deficiency makes itself felt by poverty of their moral personality, and they play a wretched part in the smallest affairs of private and professional life in which this element is called for. We recognize this type and know that many of the best clerks, distinguished by devotion to duty, expert knowledge, and exactitude belong to it. Then comes the "half," the "normal." These prove themselves to be better in the

things that even within the established channels cannot simply be "dispatched" but must also be "decided" and "carried out." Practically all business people belong here, otherwise they would never have attained their positions; most represent a selection—individually or hereditarily tested. . . . From there, rising in the scale we come finally into the highest quarter, to people who are a type characterized by super-normal qualities of intellect and will. Within this type are not only many varieties (merchants, manufacturers, financiers, etc.) but also a continuous variety of degrees of intensity in "initiative." So also the great political leader of every kind and time is a type, yet not a thing unique, but only the apex of a pyramid from which there is a continuous variation down to the average and from it to the sub-normal values.[11]

Thus, prior to and logically necessary for the conscious visions of a routinized circular flow and a dynamic entrepreneurial group, there is a deeper and more encompassing Vision of the fundamental nature of the body politic. It is comprised of a mass and an elite. The mass provides social continuity and the elite provides leadership and social change. This is the shaping Vision on which all else is built.

We are therefore back in the land of the clerks and the Carusos, generalized now to the exercise of the leadership functions by which different social classes fuflfill or fail in

---

11. Schumpeter, *Theory of Economic Development,* pp. 82–83 (slightly elided). The word "ethnically" reads "ethically," obviously a misprint, as see *Imperialism and Social Classes* (1961), p. 133. I cannot resist a delicious example of Schumpeter's deeply held beliefs as to the inherent properties of leadership. In *Business Cycles* he writes: "Sir Francis Galton's South African oxen that differed so characteristically in behavior are a good illustration of this point. Some of them went on as serenely when at the head of team as they did when at the tail of other oxen. The majority simply would not move at all when at the head." *Business Cycles,* I, p. 98, n. 1.

their social tasks at different epochs of history. "[Leadership] . . . is a special function, always clearly discernible in the actions of the individual and within the social whole. It emerges only with respect to ever new individual and social situations and would never exist if individual and national life always ran its course in the same way and by the same routine."[12]

Thus Schumpeter's Vision projects a powerful order-bestowing orientation into the flux of events. As Hoselitz points out in his introduction to Schumpeter's *Imperialism and Social Classes,* "in each case, he identifies a particular group, an elite, which under given historical and sociological conditions becomes the carrier of a movement. The carrier of economic development is the innovating entrepreneur. The carrier of imperialist ventures is . . . an aristocracy whose chief reason for existence is the ever-renewed unleashing of aggressive wars."[13] The socio-political character of society thus determines the kinds of talents that will provide it with leadership; but the distribution of talent itself will always obey the laws of statistical frequency distribution.

III

We need not further pursue the ramifications of Schumpeter's theory of elites, but must reflect on the relation between his deeper Vision and the role of economics.

Let us begin by noting a point of singular importance.

---

12. Schumpeter, *Imperialism,* p. 165. See also pp. 160–161.

13. Ibid., p. vii.

It is that the ramifications of the Vision establish the problematics of the analysis. To begin, the elitist conception of the entrepreneur removes the motive force of capitalism from the capitalist. The accumulation of capital, since Adam Smith the crucial economic activity within capitalism, is now made the consequence of the activities of economic actors *who are not themselves capitalists.* Schumpeter has previously been explicit in dissociating the businessman from any intrinsic innovatory impetus or capacity. He is equally unequivocal in dissociating the entrepreneur from the capitalist class as such. "Because being an entrepreneur is not a profession and as a rule not a lasting condition, entrepreneurs do not form a social class in the technical sense as, for example, landowners or capitalists or workingmen do."[14] Entrepreneurs seek to rise into the capitalist ranks, but they do not arise from it—at least not in significantly larger proportions than from other groups.

This separation of entrepreneurs from capitalists has two consequences for Schumpeter's subsequent economic analysis. First, it makes the process of expansion solely the outcome of exogenous forces that impinge on the system, so that the course of development and its wavelike trajectory become entirely the product of the entrepreneurial, not the capitalist function. *Thus the dynamics characteristic of capitalism arise from noncapitalist sources.* This also means that many of the constitutive elements of capitalism can be conceived without regard to their function. As we have seen, in the circular flow the capitalist exists but has

14. Schumpeter, *Theory of Economic Development,* p. 78.

no role to perform. So, too, the category of profit exists but it is not filled because profit as a value phenomenon is "fundamentally connected with the role of leadership in the economic system."[15]

We thereby arrive at the extraordinary conception of capitalism without capital. "*Capital,*" says Schumpeter in italics, "*is nothing but the lever by which the entrepreneur subjects to his control the concrete goods which he needs, nothing but a means of diverting the factors of production to new uses, or of dictating a new direction to production.*"[16] It follows that where no such lever can exist, capital must remain an empty category. What is missing from this analysis, of course, is the function served by capital in the circular flow. That function is the direction of and control over the factors of production, especially labor, in the *normal* course of economic activity. The role of capital as the medium in which power is denominated in a society of propertyless workers—the essential insight of Marx—is thereby lost to sight, and a wholly "benign" and "powerless" idea of capital becomes a central part of the preanalytic cognitive process by which the idea of capitalism is formed.

The separation of the entrepreneurial from the capitalist function has the further consequence that it removes self-expansion from the fundamental conception of the unit of capital—the business firm. The result is that competition in Schumpeter is made a product of innovation rather

---

15. Ibid., p. 147.

16. Ibid., p. 116.

than of normal business routine. Competition bears against the profits of entrepreneurs, but there is no intrinsic expansion of capital to bring pressures to bear against "normal" firms, thereby setting into motion the frenetic and inherent search for innovation and cost reduction that is part and parcel of the Marxian conception of capitalism.

In addition, it follows that there is no exploitation in the Schumpeterian model. Whether generated by new products or new processes, profit accrues entirely as "rent" to the person who has rearranged the process of production. In both cases the profit will be transient, falling again to zero as other firms move into the field or adopt the new process. This evanescent and innovation-linked aspect of profit removes all implications of exploitation, insofar as profits represent a contribution to the value of output that cannot be traced to the labor inputs of the workforce (including the "management") or to the imputed value of owned resources. Profits in a non-innovating capitalism, says Schumpeter, would be mingled with rents and wages, but would not be a phenomenon *sui generis.*[17] Hence from the beginning there is no room for the idea that an inherent feature of capitalism is a pressure of wages against profits. The conceptualization of profits as a deus ex machina that upsets the circular flow, not as an inherent force that stems from the restless efforts of capitalists to expand their socioeconomic base, entirely removes any conflictual aspect from Schumpeter's perception of capitalism.

The crucial role played by the historical Vision of natural elites makes it clear that "ideology" in Schumpeter's

---

17. Ibid., p. 147.

sense cannot be so clearly separated from "analysis" as he thought. As Maurice Dobb has put it, "*Either* the 'analysis' of which Schumpeter speaks is a purely formal structure without any relation to economic problems . . .—in which case it does not constitute a set of propositions or statements with any economic content—*or* else it is a logical system designed as the vehicle of certain statements *about* economic phenomena or activities."[18] Thus Schumpeter's Vision does not merely precede and generally shape, but enters intrinsically into the elements of the economic analysis that follows it by establishing the very terms and concepts, as well as the problematics, of that analysis. In this way moral and political judgments permeate and precede economic analysis more completely and indissolubly than Schumpeter himself thought. The idea of an inherently elitist organization of society does not entail, but powerfully predisposes that Schumpeter build his analytics from concepts that embody, or are at least compatible with, an elitist dynamic. The fully "scientific" analysis of circular flow and creative destruction can thus be traced to the heavily value-laden concepts of the rote-like businessman and the innovating entrepreneur; and this in turn can be further traced to the manifestly ideological assumption of the elite source of sociohistoric change.

Was Schumpeter himself aware of this deep Vision and the extent to which it shaped and penetrated his analytics? Perhaps, and perhaps not. The elitist vision does not have to be inferred between the lines because it is openly avowed in the very lines we have quoted. On the other

18. M. Dobb, *Theories of Value and Distribution* (1973), p. 4. His italics.

hand, Schumpeter himself did not explicitly make the connections and linkages that we have been at pains to establish. Insofar as these connections provide an analytic coherence and unity to otherwise confusing and conflicting elements in his thought, one would have supposed that Schumpeter, always the enthusiast for "analysis," would have been quick to establish these linkages, had he seen them. I will even suggest that he would not have been displeased had someone pointed them out to him.

That must perforce remain in the realm of conjecture. But it is surely worth noting that the Schumpeterian clash of visions is again reconciled by a elitist Vision in his more famous book, *Capitalism, Socialism, and Democracy.* Here the overt contradiction lies not in the tension between the inertial businessman and the dynamic entrepreneur, but in the contrast between the buoyant vista of "plausible capitalism" and the countertheme of an exhaustion of sociological morale. The first vision sets forth the stirring prospects for an entrepreneurially driven capitalism moving into a limitless horizon of technical and scientific possibilities; the second undercuts the first by its projection of a growing mood of disaffection and indifference. The contest is not, as in *The Theory of Economic Development,* between routine and innovation, but between faith and skepticism. "The bourgeois outside his office and the capitalist outside his profession cut a very sorry figure," Schumpeter writes. "Their spiritual leader is the rootless 'intellectual,' a slender reed open to every impulse and a prey to unrestrained emotionalism."[19]

---

19. Schumpeter, *Imperialism,* pp. 92–93.

From this "rootless intellectual" stems the deterioration of belief and conviction on which the system rests: "The bourgeois finds to his amazement," reads a famous sentence, "that the rationalist attitude does not stop at the credentials of kings and popes but goes on to attack private property and the whole scheme of bourgeois values."[20] The *traihison des clercs* thus brings down the magnates of capital, and the Schumpeterian scenario of economic success is brought to an ignominious conclusion by the failure of its sociological basis. But even here, the scenario is resolved by the deeper-lying Vision of elites in history. The decline of capitalism and its supersession by a sketchily described managerial socialism is regarded by Schumpeter with considerable philosophical sangfroid. And no wonder. For the managerial elite needed to direct the new socialism will be—of course—the older business elite in new uniform. Good use will be made of the "supernormal quality" of the displaced bourgeoisie.[21] Socialism will be ushered in under bourgeois auspices and will very much resemble its bourgeois antecedents.[22]

I have lingered over the Schumpeterian Vision because it is perhaps the most dramatic illustration of the manner in which "ideology" precedes and penetrates economic analysis. There is also another reason why Schumpeter's Vision is so interesting. It is that in his case, much more than in others, we are able to peer through the veils of

---

20. Schumpeter, *Capitalism, Socialism, and Democracy,* p. 143.

21. Ibid., p. 204 and 204, n. 3.

22. For a fuller discussion see my essay "Was Schumpeter Right?" in A. Heertje, ed., *Schumpeter's Vision* (1981).

personal motivation from which ideological predelictions ultimately spring. The son of middle-class parents, Schumpeter was thrust into a difficult and challenging environment when his widowed mother remarried a court general, and young Josef was dispatched to the Theresianum, a school for the children of aristocrats. By general agreement, Schumpeter internalized many of the values of this school, and throughout his life was noted for his aristocratic air.[23] This aristocratic value system is also visible in his Vision—with one difference. There the laurels are awarded to an aristocracy of talent, not of blood—to Schumpeter's own group, not to that of the scions with whom he was forced to make his private peace. Thus private orientations also inform and help us understand Schumpeter's Vision.

These intimate connections are beguiling, but not of the essence. What is of the essence is an understanding of the depth to which Visions shape and inform the undertaking of economics proper. Smith, Mill, and of course Marx, all had such Visions that defined their deepest understanding of the social processes to which they applied their analytic intelligence. We have seen how Smith's economics is built on conservative views of human behavior and relationship. Mill's political economy—above all his declarations in favor of liberty, laissez-faire, and socialism—reflect his fundamental belief in the ultimately reasonable nature and

---

23. See Christian Seidl, "Joseph Alois Schumpeter: Character, Life, and Particulars of the Graz Period," in *Lectures on Schumpeterian Economics,* Christian Seidl, ed. (1984), pp. 187–205; also Arthur Smithies, "Memorial," *American Economic Review* (1950), pp. 628–645.

developmental properties of the human being. Marx's opus also rests on a faith in human emancipation, with the difference that it sees the obstacles to development rooted in the class nature of society. So, too, we perceive the influence of these Visions in Keynes's amalgam of Burkean conservatism and Moorean idealism; in Veblen's anthropological resignation and hope; in Marshall's belief in the Victorian idea of Progress; as well as in ideas that float in the public mind to become the motivating ideologies of lesser writers. In the process by which the structure and content of social ideas are formed, the case of Joseph Schumpeter is exceptionally interesting, but not otherwise exceptional. Considerations of a Visionary kind lie behind all social theorizing, more deeply and more constitutively than we know.

8

Vision and Ideology

WHAT LIES behind the veil of economics? Vision and ideology. What does the complicated subject matter of economic analysis conceal from view? Our deep-lying, perhaps unanalyzable notions concerning human nature, history, and the like; and the various disguises by which we come to terms, especially in capitalist society, with the primary but hidden sources of social orchestration—domination and acquiesence on the one hand, affect and sociality on the other.

The reader is by now familiar with all that. Yet the problem of vision and ideology remains imperfectly examined. It lingers over these pages like an unwelcome presence, casting its shadow even when the pejorative word *ideology* has been replaced by the neutral *belief system,* or when the mystical and antiscientific term *vision* is announced as the "preanalytic cognitive act" without which the work of science cannot begin.

These are the matters that must be addressed in these final pages. If, as I deeply believe, there is no escape from the influence of visions and ideologies, then we must learn to live with them—not by abandoning all hope of examining society in a dispassionate and penetrative manner, or by resigning ourselves to becoming mere lackeys of interest and slaves of unexamined promptings, but by taking the measure of these hidden forces as best we can.

I

Let us begin by taking up the question of ideology at its worst. By "worst," I do not mean a deliberate and knowing misrepresentation or manipulation of the truth. No doubt some economists lie, as does everyone from time to time, but that is not the problem the term conjures up. Ideology, even in its extreme interpretation as lying, means *lying on behalf of an idea or an interest.* Moreover, I suspect that except in the rarest cases, lying on behalf of an interest is not performed as an act of conscious immorality, but because the ideologue is sufficiently convinced of the righteousness of his cause to justify admittedly "exaggerated" or "strictly" incorrect statements by some metamoral calculus.

Can one recognize such "blatant" ideology? I believe it is usually easy to do so, as a few examples may illustrate: In *Free to Choose,* Milton and Rose Friedman write:

> Much of the moral fervor behind the drive for equality of outcomes comes from the widespread belief that it is not fair that some children should have a great advantage over others simply because they happen to have wealthy parents. Of course it is not fair. However, unfairness can take many forms. It can take the form of inheritance of property—bonds and stocks, houses, factories; it can also take the form of the inheritance of talent—musical ability, strength, mathematical ability. The inheritance of property can be interfered with more readily than the inheri-

tance of talent. But from an ethical point of view, is there any difference between the two?[1]

The answer to their question is that there is indeed a difference. It is that we do not attach any *moral* significance to unfairnesses that arise from the dispensations of nature, whereas we do attach such significance to those imposed by society. It is not considered to be a *moral* wrong that one person is beautiful and another ugly, but the fact that one person is rich and another poor can indeed be considered a breach of morality. Thus the issue is not at all that of "equality of outcomes," but of a distinction between social, and therefore *corrigible* inequalities, and natural—presumably incorrigible—handicaps and advantages. (It follows that if plastic surgery can change ugly people into beautiful ones at acceptable cost, then beauty, like wealth, may become a candidate for moral concern.)

That which is manifestly ideological in the "worst" sense, here, is that the Friedmans would, I am certain, recognize and pounce on the flimsy nature of their argument, if it was presented to them in defense of some principle in which they disbelieved. It is their failure to apply the same degree of intellectual rigor to their own arguments as they would to those of the opposition that makes their statement an obvious example of "blatant" ideology.

A few other instances deserve mention, even if only in passing. In *The Way the World Works* Jude Wanniski

1. Milton and Rose Friedman, *Free To Choose* (1980), p. 136.

writes, "A child's principle (sic) trading partners are his parents," and "In mother and father, the child has a diversified portfolio." This "economistic" representation of human nature, which runs through the book and supports its strong free-enterprise orientation is a reductionist depiction that would put the most vulgar Marxism to shame. Yet Irving Kristol, who has a sharp eye for such reductionisms when committed in the name of Marxism, is quoted on the paperback jacket of Wanniski's book to the effect that it is the "the best economic primer since Adam Smith." Along similar lines, George Gilder tells in *Wealth and Poverty* that "capitalism begins with giving," a view that appears to change the meaning of "giving" one hundred and eighty degrees, insofar as the drive to accumulate is described by Gilder as "altruistic."

In yet another example, Robert E. Lucas, a well-known conservative theorist, makes this reply to the question of whether governments do not try to resolve social injustice: "That wouldn't be anything like my view. I can't think of explaining the pharaohs as being in existence to resolve the social injustice in Egypt. I think they perpetrated most of the social injustice in Egypt." The point at issue is not whether the pharaohs were, in fact, the perpetrators of most of the injustice in ancient Egypt, but why "government" conjures up pharaonic Egypt for Lucas, not Lincolnian America. I leave the worst of the worst for last: Gordon Tullock, writing on the *Economics of Income Redistribution,* ranks the United States's crop-restriction programs "with the work of Stalin, Hitler, and Mao among the major mass murder programs of our time." A reviewer in the *Journal of Economic Literature* writes of this claim, "[E]ven slight damage would be hard to prove. For Tullock's unsupported claim of mass murder (which implies also intent), the irresponsibility is enormous."[2]

In all these instances, ideology is readily enough identifiable either by its indifference to the generally recognized facts of economic or social or political life, its manifestly weak or question-begging logic, or by its reckless overstatement. Of course we find precisely the same flaws in the blatant ideologies of socialism as in those of capitalism. In one case as in the other, however, there is no reason to fear that ideology ineluctably pushes its spokesmen into excesses of apologism or polemic. It is possible to present beliefs, no matter how passionately held, in a manner that weighs evidence, considers alternatives, and makes assertions as hypotheses, not dogma. Indeed, the strongest belief statements usually have this quality of modesty and diffidence which immeasurably strengthens their plausibility.[3]

II

Blatant ideology is thus not the aspect of the veil of economics that I find interesting or important. Of far greater consequence are statements that have none of these egregious defects but that must nonetheless be revealed as "ideological" because they can be shown to be

---

2. Jude Wanniski, *The Way the World Works* (1978), pp. 47, 49; George Gilder, *Wealth and Poverty* (1981), p. 21f; Lucas quoted in Arjo Klamer, *Conversations with Economists* (1984), p. 52. Gordon Tullock, *Economics of Income Redistribution* (1983), p. 164, reviewed by Jerome Rothenberg in the *Journal of Economic Literature* (March 1987), p. 118.

3. For an example, I cite Peter L. Berger, *The Capitalist Revolution* (1986).

false or contradictory, *although not wittingly so.*

Let me again illustrate the problem with a few examples. A generally held idea of conventional economics is that its fundamental conceptual building block is the idea of the "rational, maximizing individual." In my initial chapter I have dealt with some of the empirical difficulties that attend the use of "rational" and "maximizing," but let us now consider a more fundamental difficulty that reveals the unexamined nature of the premise on which the concept is reared.

The key word is "individual." Virtually the first act the individual is called on to perform—in a hundred textbooks, not in life—is the rational, maximizing allocation of his or her income. What is the problem here? It is that *income* is intrinsically a social concept, whereas "individual" is intrinsically a nonsocial one. There can be no "income" in a Robinson Crusoe economy of a single individual. No doubt a solitary person can apportion his energies as he wishes, including in a rational and maximizing fashion, but energies are not "income"—if they were, all energetic individuals would be rich without further ado. (Many texts compound the conceptual problem by asking the individual to allocate his *wages*—introducing a class term as well as a social one.)[4]

What we have here is a logical lapse that is not recognized as such. Morever, even if it were so recognized, its power of belief conversion is small. I cannot imagine a conventional economist, who may have just encountered for the first time the illogicality of the premise of the

4. See Ben Fine, *Theories of the Capitalist Economy* (1982), pp. 16–17.

income-allocating "individual," renouncing his confidence in the belief structure of economics that is erected on that concept. The interests that this structure serves are too broad and deep to be dispelled by mere disproof. Belief structures linger on, almost impervious to fact or logic, because they allay the "tumult of the imagination"—the anxiety, we would say—that Adam Smith cogently identified as the primary need to which theorizing addresses itself.[5]

As I have written elsewhere, this stubborn persistence of value judgments arises because the economist does not engage in his analysis from a wholly disinterested position, indifferent to the conclusions to which his analysis may lead:

> [T]he social investigator is inextricably bound up with the objects of his scrutiny, as a member of a group, a class, a society, a nation, bringing with him feelings of animus or defensiveness to the phenomenon he observes. In a word, his position in society—not only his material position, but his moral position—is implicated in and often jeopardized by the act of investigation, and it is not surprising, therefore, that behind the great bulk of social science we find arguments that serve to justify the existential position of the social scientists.[6]

There are many examples of the staying power of belief systems despite their internal weaknesses. Perhaps the best known of these is the conflation of the physical agencies of land and resources with the social claims of "Land"

---

5. Adam Smith, "The History of Astronomy," in *Essays in Philosophical Subjects* (1980), pp. 45–46.

6. R. Heilbroner, *An Inquiry into the Human Prospect,* 2nd ed. (1980), p. 21.

and "Capital." At least since the time of John Stuart Mill, economists have understood the difference between the contribution of actual land and resources to production and the claims of their owners to a share in the product. The fact is, however, that economists continue to anthropomophize property, speaking of land and capital as if they were embodiments of will and energy who would not perform their tasks if "they" (not their owners) were not motivated or rewarded by income. In this way, "land, labor, and capital" are identified as the "factors of production," thereby tacitly eliding the crucial social difference between labor and property.

It is in this manner that economics spreads its ideological veil over capitalism, shielding from inspection its regimelike character and allowing us to see instead a depoliticized and desocialized "price system." The belief-systems by which we perceive capitalism in this manner present for our analysis very different kinds of problems from those that would strike us if we perceived it as otherwise. By screening out all aspects of domination and acquiescence, as well as those of affect and trust, it encourages us to understand capitalism as fundamentally "economic"—not social or political—in nature. Indeed, as we have seen, it establishes the concept of "economics" itself as a mode of social articulation that is separated from—not built atop—older modes of social orchestration.

III

I have said that ideology penetrates and permeates economics, not because its telltale signs cannot be discerned, but because its capacity to allay the need for a value framework cannot readily be overcome.

Is there then no possibility of throwing off the biases and prejudices—in politer words, the value judgments—of ideology? Must economics, of necessity, always bear the marks of its subservience to a social order? Is the invocation of science as the ideal of economics no more than a chimera—worse, a pious self-deception?

I do not ask these questions rhetorically, to set the stage for a ringing defense of economics-as-science. If my preceding argument has any validity, it makes impossible such a last minute resort to intellectual patriotism. Ideology is *part* of economics—not the whole, but a constitutive part. Its motivations are not only powerful, indeed inescapable, but legitimate. We cannot expect the commandments of scientific discipline to override these considerations, especially insofar as science itself is not immune to protecting its belief systems from a confrontation with unwelcome ideas.[7]

What, then, can be said? I shall make a few points that will not remove the problem of ideology—it is irremovable—but that may make it easier to accept and to use constructively:

1. As these very essays show, it is possible to construct alternative ideologies. The alternative views are certainly not themselves immune from the charge of being "ideological" in their nature—that is, of containing arguable premises, perhaps internal inconsistencies. The historical basis or bias of my own views can readily be challenged. The

7. See Paul Feyerabend, *Against Method* (1975), passim.

centrality of power and affect, crucial to my discussion, can certainly be contested. The interpretation of the market system as a mode of social integration that conceals older forms of social discipline is equally open to disagreement or rejection. What is important is to agree that more than one set of conceptual elements can be formulated to explicate the problems to which economists set their minds. Thus no single reading can be adjudged the Truth. I emphasize this statement because I sometimes fear that economists more than scientists yield to the temptation of asserting their belief systems as *true* belief systems. That simple admission of fallibility, consciously held and vigorously maintained, is enough to loosen, although not to untie, the constraints that ideology imposes.

2. The tasks of science and ideology are different. Science is concerned with the testing of theories about the empirical world. Its reach does not extend to the creation of the conceptual units by which that world assumes its "empirical" form. Science concerns our comprehension of how the world functions, not of how we perceive it in the first place. As the example of modern physics makes clear, science often busies itself with concepts whose "meaning"—even whose "existence"—is only a mental convenience to allow theorizing to take place: thus we have "particles" that have "color," "charm," "strangeness," and the like.

With economics too, the reach of economic science cannot extend to the matter of concept formation. Such building blocks of economic theory as "individuals" or "society," "utility" or "value," "labor" or "capital," are created by observers from the protean stuff of the external world and inner promptings. They are, if you will, "metaphysical,"[8] or perhaps better, heuristic. As we have seen, these concepts may lead to logical contradictions or paradoxes, or they may have no operational usefulness. On the basis of science and logic they should therefore be discarded, and replaced by other constructions and conceptions. None of them, however, will ever be able to claim science as its paternity. The mother and father of all social constructs remain of necessity the human being who is driven to "discover" concepts in order to come to terms with its existential plight. Of necessity, these concepts must embody the value-laden elements that is their primary raison d'être.

3. Such an acknowledgment does not remove ideology but legitimates it, and defines its task vis-à-vis that of science. Ideology, or belief systems to give them their more acceptable name, provide us with the comprehension by which the "natural" world is identified as such. Science then explores and examines the empirical data that *this particular set of values identifies,* constructs theories from the data that have been designated as relevant, tests these theories, usually by examining the robustness of their predictive implications, and reassesses, or alters, or even abandons its beliefs if the theories fail to yield useful results.

We mainly discover this application of science in the open and inquiring stance with which most economists approach the "workings" of the system. I put the word into quotes, however, because the workings refer almost

8. See Joan Robinson, *Economic Philosophy* (1962), ch. 1.

exclusively to movements on the surface of the economy—what I have described as its "market" aspect—rather than inquiring into the social and political depths below—my concept of a "regime." That is why economics manages, with an admirable composure, to take up and discard one "theory" after another—monetarism, supply-side economics, rational expectations, and whatever will come next—and that is why it elevates this willingness to try on and discard theories like clothing, as testifying to the scientific status of the discipline.

That which remains unacknowedged, as I have tried to make clear, is the substratum of beliefs that causes us to structure our perceptions in terms of an "economy" rather than a sociopolitical order; or to see "individuals" rather than individuated social beings; or two realms rather than a single unstably constituted regime. If I am correct that capitalism is moving through a period of difficult adjustment, perhaps the discrepancies and inadequacies of its regnant belief system will intensify, leading to a differently constituted, more historical and self-scrutinizing set of conceptual building blocks. But that is no more than a possibility. Dogma and increasingly rigid orthodoxy are responses to challenge as much as reflection and adaptation.

IV

The question of how a social order might respond to challenges against its belief system brings us to the question of vision—our deepest, often only half-consciously held notions with respect to such vast but vague ideas as "human nature" or "society," "history" or "progress."

Visions differ from ideologies in at least two significant ways. The first is that they are never falsifiable in the sense in which at least some ideological concepts can be shown up as partial construals of reality (pharaohs as government) or excessive description (crop restriction as mass murder). In the visionary rather than ideological preface to inquiry, we treat human behavior or social existence as "tendencies." No appeal to past or present experience can confirm or disconfirm these statements. Our visions are concerned with such matters as the inherent orientation of human society toward hierarchy or toward equality; the pacific or aggressive "nature" of the human species being, and its capabilities for socialization; the resemblance of social systems to biological orders;[9] and yet other fundamental preconceptions about social reality. Such general preconceptions that cannot be proved or disproved—or worse, can all too easily be "proved" or "disproved" by appeal to historical example or introspection. History and introspection will provide some support for many such general assertions, but it will also yield evidence for contrary kinds of generalization. This is because the human psyche is itself full of contradictions, all aspects of which are mirrored in historical experience. There is no way of claiming precedence for one aspect of the psyche over another—love over hate, conformity over individuation, even self-interest over affect. Visions remain visionary.

Second, our visions, unlike our ideological beliefs, never contain logical contradictions. This is because they are constructed at too high a level of abstraction to entail

---

9. See Hirshleifer, "Expanding Domain of Economics."

illogical consequences. The perception of history as progress or stasis or decline, of society as necessitously hierarchical or tendentially egalitarian, of human nature itself as given or made, not only defy all laboratory concepts of "testing," but give rise to no paradoxes or logical flaws. Visions are not logical constructs.

At this deepest level of social inquiry our analytic and expository powers diminish almost to the vanishing point. We can say very little as to the sources of these constellations that we project into the social universe. Few of us can trace to their social or personal roots the experiences that frame our own visions. Why each becomes radical or conservative, reformist or cynical, optimist or pessimist remains, in general, a problem of near impenetrable complexity—or worse, a problem whose profound importance and elusive character do not even enter our minds.

Yet there is little doubt at to the immense constructive power of our visions. Schumpeter is right: without vision there can be no analysis. There will be nothing to analyze. There will be no "world," no "problems," no "tendencies," no possibilities. My central placement of ideology and vision is therefore not intended as a retreat to a hopelessly personal or pointlessly reductionist view of economic inquiry. There is ample room for economic analysis, indispensable for unraveling the movements of a capitalist system. But the analysis cannot begin without the conceptual units of a belief system; and this belief system, in turn, must reflect the nature of the human adventure as we half-consciously—perhaps wholly unconsciously—understand it. Thus it is not to diminish the idea of economics that I seek to reveal ideology and vision beneath its veil. If ideology is to be criticized, vision is to be celebrated. Values come first in our search for meaning in history and society. Too often a vehicle for mystification, economics can best become an instrument for enlightenment if we see it as the means by which we strive to make a workable science out of morality.

Index

accumulation, of capital, 66
  failures of, 56–58, 72–73, 146–47
  as a motivation in Smith's system, 135–38
  social structure of, 60–61, 67
  see also wealth
acquiescence:
  in nonmarket societies, 19, 20
  and power, 31
Africa, ancient kingdoms of, 69
altruism, 26–28
Amin, Samir, 64–65
anthropology, and nonmarket societies, 18–19. *See also* society
Appleby, Joyce, 28–29
Aquinas, St. Thomas, 49, 109
Arendt, Hannah, 100
Aristotle, 49, 88, 100–101, 109, 111
Arrighi, Giovanni, 64–65
Arrow, Kenneth, 128

barter, 23–24
behavior:
  and individual freedom, 21–23
  in market societies, 24–27
  and nonmarket societies, 18–20, 24
  rational, 25–27, 46–47
belief systems, *see* ideology
Bentham, Jeremy, 49
Böhm-Bawerk, Eugen, 123
Braudel, Fernand, 50
Business Cycles (Schumpeter), 172

calculation, rational, 25–26, 33, 47
Calvin, John, 89
capital:
  anthropomorphization of, 192
  capitalism without, 178–79
  drive for, 36–37
  and the entrepreneur, 177–79
  and power, 30
  substitution for labor of, 52–53
Capital (Marx), 124, 134, 149, 150
capitalism, 8, 34, 35
  allocation of resources in, 53
  without capital, 178–79
  and cultural change, 46–50
  cycles in, 64–65
  and the entrepreneur, 170–73, 177–79
  external motions in, 54–59, 73
  failures in accumulation process, 57–58
  and freedom, 99–100
  historical view of, 41–50, 59–61
  and ideology, 47–50, 72
  institutional structures, 60–61, 65
  internal logic of, 50–53
  momentum in, 65
  money–commodity–money

Index

capitalism *(continued)*
(M–C–M′) circuit, 37, 38, 51, 55, 56, 58, 59–61
motivations in, 135–36
political *vs.* economic activity in, 43–45, 71, 73–74, 76, 138–41
and population, 152–53
power in, 29–31, 38–39
and problems of scale, 161–62
profit in, 39–41
and rationality, 46–47
as a regime, 35, 37–38, 41, 59, 67
Smith's logic of, 141–51, 159–61
and state socialism, 77–79
stationary state of, 167–70, 171–73
and technology, 147–52, 154–57, 160–64
and value, 107
and wealth, 35–41, 135–36
and work, 89–93, 96–99
as a world system, 73, 75
see also market system
Capitalism, Socialism, and Democracy (Schumpeter), 181
China, ancient, 69, 70, 75
Christianity, 88–89
civilization:
and exploitation, 87, 102
and work, 87, 102
Clark, J. B., 109
class:
and division of society, 71, 137
and ideology, 47–48
and power, 30
and Schumpeter's view of history, 174–76
command, 15–16, 17, 33
and market system, 21
and nonmarket societies, 19, 22
commodities, and wealth, 36–37
Communist Manifesto, The (Marx and Engels), 36
competition, 51, 168, 178–79
costs and benefits, 47
cost-of-production theory of value, 116–20, 129
craftsman, 87–88
crisis, economic, 66–67, 72–73
custom, *see* tradition

Deane, Phyllis, 153–54
Debreu formulation, 128
demand, saturation of, 146–47
distribution, in nonmarket societies, 17–18
division of labor, 97, 143–45
and technology, 154–57
Dobb, Maurice, 180
domestic mode of production, 81, 84–85
replacement of, 85–86
Dynamics of a Global Crisis (Wallerstein, Frank, Amin, and Arrighi), 64–65

economics:
definitions of, 13–15, 32–34
heuristics in, 195
historical view of, 66, 68, 70–72
and inquiry, 106–7
and Schumpeter's analysis, 179–81
as science, 180, 193, 194–96
vision in, 197–99
Economics of Income Redistribution (Tullock), 188–89
Edgeworth, Francis Ysidro, 127
Egypt, ancient, 36, 69, 70, 75
elites, Schumpeter's theory of, 174–76, 179–81
employment, 39, 89
and subordination, 96–99
see also labor and labor force; work
Engels, Friedrich, 36, 99, 158

England, 43, 61
English revolution, 42
Enlightenment, The, 159
enterprise, size distributions of, 56–57
entrepreneurship, 170–73, 177–79
Erikson, Erik H., 18*n*–19*n*
Essay on Civil Society, An (Ferguson), 156
Europe, feudal, 70
exchange, 23–29, 34
  first appearance of, 22
  and power, 29–31
  relationship, 24–25
  value, 111–14
exploitation:
  rents and profits as, 91–92
  in Schumpeter's model, 179
  work as, 86–87, 102

Fascism, 78
Ferguson, Adam, 156
Frank, Andre Gunder, 64–65
freedom, 21–23, 73, 135
  and private property, 45–46
  and socialism, 79
  and work, 80–81, 85, 90, 96, 98–99, 103
Free to Choose (Friedman and Friedman), 186–87
French revolution, 42
Freud, Sigmund, 19*n*, 100
Friedman, Milton, 186–87
Friedman, Rose, 186–87

General Motors, 77, 79
General Theory (Keynes), 172
German Ideology, The (Marx and Engels), 99
gift giving, 23
Gilder, George, 188
Godelier, Maurice, 14*n*
Gordon, David, 60
Gossen, Herma
Great Depressio
gross national pro
  54–56, 129
growth, economic: in
  56–58

Hahn, Frank, 128
heuristics, in economic the
Hirsch, Fred, 27–28
Hirschman, Albert, 49
Hobbes, Thomas, 95
Holland, 61
Horvat, Branko, 78–79
Hoselitz, Bert, 176

ideology:
  blatant, 186–89
  conservative, 130
  in economics, 13–14, 32, 185, 193–96
  logical lapses as a result of, 189–92
  and rise of capitalism, 47–50
  and vision, 166–67, 173, 182–84, 197, 198–99
Imperialism and Social Classes (Schumpeter), 176
impersonality, in market society, 24–25, 29, 38
Incas, 75, 76
India, 75–76
individuals:
  in conventional economic theories, 190–91
  freedom of, 21–23
  in market society, 16, 21–22, 24–29, 30–31, 33
  in nonmarket societies, 19–20
  and power, 29–31
  and rationality, 26–28
interchange, in nonmarket societies, 23–24

Jevons, W. S., 115–16, 126
Journal of Economic Literature, 188–89
justice, 110*n*

Keynes, John Maynard, 62, 172, 184
Keynesian economics, 67
Kirzner, Israel, 14*n*
Kondratief cycle, 64–65
Kristol, Irving, 188
!Kung society, 82

labor and labor force:
  cheap, 77
  contractual, 39, 89
  disutility of, 113
  division of, 97, 143–45
  and exchange value, 111–14
  and freedom, 45–46, 90–92, 135
  Marx on, 22, 120–22
  and power, 30
  propertyless, 43
  Smith on, 141–47
  and standard of living, 153–54, 156–59
  substitution of capital for, 52–53
  and technology, 154–57
  and value, 105, 111–17, 118
  and work, 89–92, 97
labor power, 121
labor theory of value, 105, 111–16, 122
land:
  anthropomorphization of, 192
  Marx on, 22
  and power, 30
  see also property, private
Locke, John, 28–29, 49, 130
Lowe, Adolph, 16*n,* 109, 148
Lucas, Robert E., 188
Luther, Martin, 88–89

Making of the English Working Class, The (Thompson), 158
market system, 15–17
  empirical study of, 32
  and ideology, 33
  impersonality in, 24
  individual freedom in, 21–23
  integrative process in, 16–17, 22–23
  power in, 29–31
  rationality and motivation in, 24–27, 46–47
  relationship between employer and labor in, 39–40
  rise of, 42–43
Marshall, Alfred, 39, 126
Marx, Karl, 7, 8, 22, 50, 51, 58, 106, 119, 134, 137, 158, 164, 178, 183, 184
  on capitalism and capitalist societies, 36–37, 61–62, 99
  on exploitation, 92
  on value, 120–25
Marxian economics:
  and power in market systems, 29–30, 40
  and value, 120–25, 132–33
maximizing behavior, 27, 113, 190
Methodenstreit, 104
Mill, John Stuart, 50, 61, 147, 164, 167, 183–84, 192
money–commodity–money (M–C–M′) circuit, 37, 38, 51, 55, 56, 58, 59–61
Montaigne, Michel de, 47
morality:
  and economics, 34, 49–50
  and ideology, 187
  and value, 108–11
  and work, 88–89
motivation:
  accumulation of capital as, 135–36

of the entrepreneur, 177–79
in market system, 21–22, 24–27, 33
in nonmarket societies, 18
power as, 136
routine and custom as, 169–70
for work, 93–96

nonmarket systems, 17–20, 22
interchange in, 23–24

Pareto, Vilfredo, 109
philanthropy, 27
Plato, 88
Polanyi, Karl, 17–18
Political Economy of Socialism, The (Horvat), 78–79
politics, and economics, 33
and rise of market society, 42–43, 43–44, 71
Smith's view of, 138–41
and value, 110–11
Politics (Aristotle), 111
population, 147, 152–53
Posner, Richard A., 14*n*
power, 7, 29–31
historical transfer of, 41–43
as a motivation, 136
national, 42
negative, 38–39
and work, 87, 94–95
price systems, 7, 16, 111–12. *See also* value
price theory, *see* utility theory of value
Prisoner's Dilemma, 26
production:
control of, 41, 44
centralized mode of, 85–90, 100
domestic mode of, 81, 84–85, 100
and labor theory of value, 114–16
means of, 30, 38
modes of, 16
in nonmarket societies, 17–18, 84
surplus, 36
technological mode of, 101
productivity, historical view of, 76–77
profit:
and rents, 90–91, 168, 172
in Schumpeter's model, 179
and value, 116–17, 119
and wages, 52–53
property, private:
and freedom, 45–46
and labor, 39, 45–46
in means of production, 38–39
and power, 30, 136–37
rents and profits from, 90–81
withholding of, 38–39
in workless societies, 84–85
provisioning of societies, 14–15, 20, 32–33, 105–6
public sector, enlargement of, 56
Pygmy society, 82

rationality, 26–28, 190
and calculation, 25–26, 33
and rise of capitalism, 46–47
Rawls, John, 110*n*
Reagan, Ronald, 66
Reaganomics, 63–64, 66
regime, 35, 37–38, 196
religion:
and ideology, 72
and market behavior, 27–28
rents, 90–91, 116–17, 119, 168, 172
requital, equality of, 24
Ricardo, David, 61, 147, 164, 167
on value, 111–12, 114, 115, 116, 118–19, 123, 124
Roman Empire, 75
Rostow, W. W., 151
Rüstow, Alexander, 86

Sahlins, Marshall, 81
Schumpeter, Joseph, 8, 39, 46, 50, 51, 62, 110, 145, 198
economic model of, 165–84
science, economics as, 180, 193, 194–96
Second Treatise on Government (Locke), 49
self-interest, 25–26
Sharpe, Myron, 63*n*
Smith, Adam, 7, 8, 39, 40, 46, 61, 177, 183, 191
capitalism of, 134–64. *See also* capitalism
on centralized mode of production, 90, 96–97
logic of capitalism, 141–47
on relation of government to economy, 138–41
on rents and profits, 91–92
on value, 111, 112–13, 114, 115, 116, 117–19, 120, 124, 125
on wealth, 36, 94, 95
socialism, state, 77–79
socialization, in nonmarket societies, 18–20, 22
society:
capitalist, 35–36, 70
desires in, 37
economic, 13–14
exchange in, 23–29
and ideology, 47–48
market, 16–17, 21–29
nonmarket, 17–20, 22
power in, 29–31, 42
precapitalist, 36, 38, 41, 70
primitive, 17–20, 81–85
provisioning of, 14–15, 20, 32–33, 105–6
roles in, 18, 70–71, 87–88, 174–76
and work, 83–89
Socrates, 88
Sraffa, Piero, 124
standards of living, 153–54, 156–59
Stigler, George J., 118
subordination, and work, 85–89, 96–99, 100–101
success, 95–96, 100
surplus:
generation of, 69–70, 76–77
"sharing" of, 137
Sweden, 78

Taiwan, 77
technology:
and Smith's capitalism, 147–52, 154–57, 160–64
and work, 100–101
Theory of Economic Development (Schumpeter), 167, 181
Theory of Justice, A (Rawls), 110*n*
Thompson, E. P., 158
Tocqueville, Alexis de, 157
tradition, 15–16, 17, 22, 33
and market systems, 21
Tragedy of the Commons, 26
Trobiander society, 82
Tullock, Gordon, 188–89

utility maximization, 37
utility theory of value, 126–30

value, 104–5
cost-of-production theory of, 116–20, 129
equal exchange of, 24, 29
general problematic of, 105–8, 130–33
labor theory of, 105, 111–16
Marxian theory of, 120–25, 132–33
normative approach to, 108–11
surplus, 40
theory, 107–8
utility theory of, 126–30
and wealth, 36

Veblen, Thorstein Bunde, 50, 184
vision, 165–66, 185, 196–99
  and ideology, 166–67, 173, 182–84, 197, 198–99

wages, and profit, 52–53
Wallerstein, Immanuel, 64–65, 73
Walras, Léon, 127
Wanniski, Jude, 187–88
Way the World Works, The (Wanniski), 187–88
wealth:
  accumulation of, 35–37, 67
  generation of, 69–70
  and GNP, 54–55
  and rational behavior, 46–47
  and work, 84
Wealth and Poverty (Gilder), 188
Wealth of Nations, The (Smith), 61, 111, 135, 137, 139, 141, 143–44, 149, 150, 155, 159–61
Weber, Max, 46, 50
work, 82–83
  and capitalism, 89–92
  denigration of, 88
  as an expression of freedom, 80–81, 101–2, 103
  motivation for, 93–96
  and morality, 88–89
  in primitive societies, 81–85
  as subordination, 85–89, 96–99
  a world without, 100–103
work ethic, 88–89

Yir-Yoront society, 82, 83